The 10 Things You Need to Know About Sex Addiction

An Essential Guide for Partners, Individuals, and Professionals

by:

Dr. Chris Samuels

**The 10 Things You Need to Know About Sex Addiction:
An Essential Guide for Partners, Individuals, and Professionals**

Copyright © 2025 by Dr. Chris Samuels

Published in the United States

ISBN: 979-8-9932815-1-3

All rights reserved. No part of this publication may be reproduced, stored in a retrieval system, or transmitted by any means, electronic, mechanical, photocopy, recording, or otherwise, without the author's prior permission except as provided by Australian copyright law.

The names, characters, and stories presented in this book are used fictitiously. Any resemblance to actual people, living or deceased, or real-life events is purely coincidental. The examples and scenarios are intended solely for illustrative and educational purposes.

Dedication

This book is dedicated to the countless men and women, individuals, couples, and families, who had the courage to seek treatment for sexual addiction when society offered only shame and judgment.

In choosing healing over hiding, you pioneered a march from the shadows of societal shame toward the healing light of acceptance and understanding. You trusted me with your most vulnerable truths and, in doing so, became my greatest teachers. Everything I came to know that could be of help to others, I learned first from you.

I am also deeply grateful to Madeline Breckinridge, whose unwavering support and wisdom enhanced my growth in this field at every step, and to the brilliant Linda Reed-Enever, who helped me find my voice when I needed it most.

To all who walk the path of recovery and to those who support them on that journey, this work is yours as much as mine.

About the Author

I'm Dr. Chris Samuels, a licensed clinical psychologist and Certified Sexual and Relational Therapist (CSRTT) with more than 30 years specializing in sexual addiction treatment and in helping partners heal from betrayal trauma. My work has focused on guiding individuals and couples as they navigate the profound challenges that emerge when sexual addiction is discovered, with the understanding that both partners need support and compassionate care during this critical time. I was among the first clinicians to recognize that sexual addiction typically has its roots in childhood trauma and attachment wounds, and that effective treatment must address these underlying issues rather than focusing solely on behavioral change. This perspective, now increasingly recognized in the field, has shaped my clinical approach and my training of other professionals.

Throughout my career, I have been committed not only to treating individuals and couples but also to expanding the field's capacity to serve those affected by sexual addiction. Through the Sexual Addiction Treatment and Training Institute (SATTI), which I founded in 1992 and continue to direct, I have trained hundreds of clinicians in trauma-based approaches to sexual addiction and betrayal trauma. I am currently completing two additional books that will build on this work, furthering my mission to bring clarity, validation, and effective treatment approaches to everyone impacted by sexual addiction.

Contents

Introduction	7
1. What Exactly Is Sex Addiction?	11
2. Isn't Sex Addiction Just Another Name for Promiscuity?	22
3. What's the Difference Between Someone Who Is a Sex Addict and Someone Who Just Has a Normally High Sex Drive?	26
4. From Behaviors to Impact: The Full Scope of Sexual Addiction	30
5. Breaking the Gender Myth: Sexual Addiction Affects Both Men and Women	45
6. What Are the Signs and Symptoms to Look for in a Person Who Is a Sex Addict?	52
7. What About the Spouses and Partners of Sex Addicts? What Is Their Story?	61
8. Is There Treatment for Sexual Addiction?	69
9. With Alcoholism, You Just Give Up the Drug. What Do You Do with Sex Addiction . . . Give Up Sex?	99
10. Isn't Sexuality a Private Matter? Why Should We Care Whether or Not Someone Is a Sex Addict?	115

Introduction

This guide is designed for anyone seeking clarity about sex addiction, whether you're a clinician encountering this issue in your practice, a student learning about this addiction for the first time, a partner grappling with betrayal trauma, or someone struggling with sexual compulsivity yourself. Beyond individual understanding, this guide also addresses why sexual addiction requires broader societal attention through education and public health initiatives, as this is an issue that also affects our entire society.

In my three decades specializing in the treatment of sexual addiction and betrayal trauma, I have witnessed the widespread confusion surrounding this condition across all these groups. I've observed how the lack of clear information leaves clinicians feeling unprepared to help, students without essential knowledge about a pervasive problem, partners questioning their reality and blaming themselves, and those struggling with sexual compulsivity trapped in shame and the belief that they are simply weak-willed for failing to solve this problem through willpower alone. Our society does little more to address it than make lame jokes about it or conflate it with an occasional sensationalized scandal.

Through my work training hundreds of mental health professionals in this specialty, I've seen firsthand how this knowledge gap affects treatment outcomes and perpetuates suffering across all affected populations. This is particularly concerning given the widespread impact of pornography addiction, a major component of sex addiction, which is increasingly affecting individuals, relationships, and families as access becomes more ubiquitous and content becomes more extreme. Whether you're seeking to understand these issues professionally or personally, this guide aims to provide the clarity and validation essential for healing and effective intervention.

The degree of confusion surrounding sex addiction is not surprising, since both sex and addiction are often controversial topics. When the two words are put together, sex addition, they create room for wildly differing viewpoints that can be especially harmful for anyone seeking help, whether that's therapists trying to treat clients, partners trying to understand what's happening in their relationships, or individuals struggling with compulsive sexual behavior trying to understand their own experience. This confusion prevents people from getting the specialized care they need and perpetuates stigma across all affected groups.

Because sex addiction was a relatively new field when I first encountered it, it's primarily my clients—both those with the addiction and their partners—who have taught me about the realities of this condition: the early histories that create vulnerability, the pathway to becoming addicted to sex, the distorted lives lived in addiction, and the enormous consequences the addiction exacts on partners, families, and even employers.

In my experience, I observed that almost without exception, individuals with sexual addiction shared several distinctive commonalities in their childhood years that were signs of neglect and abuse in their home environments. These common factors reflected a significant lack of many of the essentials a child needs to grow and prosper: dependable nurturance, available, reliable, and intimate attachment opportunities, sheltering from physical, emotional, or sexual abuse, and secure parental boundaries.

For these individuals, their sex addiction was an almost logical development, starting as it did as a misguided attempt to meet those essential unmet needs and to numb the pain that accompanies trauma and neglect. Unfortunately, as with all addictions, what starts as a problem-solver eventually becomes the problem, as the addiction takes over more and more of the person's life in increasingly destructive ways to them and all those around them.

Understanding this context is crucial for anyone affected by sexual addiction. For partners, recognizing that the addiction isn't about you, your worthiness, or your adequacy can begin the healing process from betrayal trauma. For those struggling with sexual compulsivity, understanding these developmental origins can help lift the burden of shame and the belief that you are simply weak-willed. For clinicians, recognizing these dynamics is essential for effective treatment, as traditional addiction models often fall short when they don't address underlying trauma and attachment wounds.

For anyone in recovery from sexual addiction, if he or she is to move beyond merely "stopping bad behaviors" and instead move forward into transformative recovery, where healthy attachment and intimacy become possible, the early trauma must be a focus. While stopping compulsive behaviors is essential, ongoing treatment must focus on healing the underlying, unresolved trauma that helped establish the addiction and continues to maintain it.

My treatment philosophy, developed through decades of clinical work and training other professionals, recognizes that sexual addiction is a complex condition requiring specialized understanding. Partners neither caused the addiction nor can control it. Those struggling with sexual compulsivity are not weak or immoral: they are dealing with a legitimate condition with identifiable causes and effective treatments. Clinicians need specific training to provide the informed support essential for healing across all affected individuals. And, given the widespread impact of sexual addiction on individuals, families, and communities, our mental health agencies must address the need for public health initiatives that focus on prevention, early intervention, and accessible treatment resources.

Whether you're seeking to understand this issue professionally, personally, or as a societal concern, this guide aims to provide clarity about sexual addiction's true nature, lifting shame, providing validation, and promoting the serious, compassionate approach this condition deserves.

Christine Samuels, Ph.D., CPSBT, CSRTT
Founder and Director (1992)
Sexual Addiction Treatment and Training Institute (SATTI)
thesattigroup.com | drchrissamuels.com

1. What Exactly Is Sex Addiction?

There have been lots of sensational headlines about it recently, especially attached to famous names, lots of lame jokes when mention of it comes up in conversation, and even debates among mental health professionals about whether it even exists or is just a psychobabble excuse for bad behavior–or maybe even a new way for greedy clinicians to make a living.

The skepticism is understandable. We live in a culture that simultaneously hypersexualizes everything while maintaining deep ambivalence about sexuality itself. When a politician, athlete, or celebrity is caught in a sex scandal, the "sex addiction" explanation often sounds like a convenient public relations move, and of course they'll soon be "getting treatment." The timing of these revelations—usually right after getting caught—doesn't add to the credibility of the diagnosis.

But let me tell you what sex addiction actually looks like when it walks through my office door. It doesn't arrive with fanfare or excuses. It walks in quietly, often after years of private struggle, carrying a burden of shame so profound that many clients can barely make eye contact during their first session.

The Reality Behind Closed Doors

Meet Tom. He came for help because he had been married for six months, to "the woman of his dreams," as he described her, but despite his love for her, he had continued his longstanding pattern of infidelity. Starting in high school, with his first real girlfriend, and continuing right up to the second week of his new marriage, he had never been able to remain faithful to a woman he loved. Not even the guilt and shame that his behavior had always engendered in him stopped him. He had become expert at keeping his behavior hidden or, when, in the past it had been discovered, making promises, which he sincerely believed, to never engage in that behavior again. But his promises were not a sufficient bulwark against his compulsive need to win over his next sexual conquest, to be admired and be the focus of the next adoring woman.

This time, though, neither promises nor lies were successful in convincing his new wife that her discovery of his infidelity could be forgiven or resolved. Although he had long been aware of the negative nature of his behavior, this was the first time that he realized the depth of pain that his betrayal had caused someone he truly loved. And he was now faced with the possibility of losing her, despite their love for each other. This was what finally brought Tom into treatment.

When he first sat in my office, his hands shook as he tried to explain his behavior. "I know how this sounds," he said, "but I love my wife more than anything. I would never want to hurt her. But I can't seem to stop myself." His voice broke as he described the look on his wife's face when she discovered his latest betrayal, a look he said haunted him every night since.

Tom's pattern had been escalating for over a decade. What started as occasional infidelity in high school had evolved into an elaborate system of dating apps, secret phone numbers, and carefully orchestrated lies. He had developed what we call "addiction-supporting behaviors," the complex web of deception necessary to maintain the addiction. He kept separate email accounts, a secret second phone, had memorized the schedules of potential partners, and had become masterful at reading people's vulnerabilities to exploit them for sexual conquest.

The neurochemical rush he got from the pursuit was as powerful as any drug. Brain imaging studies indeed show that the same reward pathways activated by cocaine and alcohol light up during the anticipation and pursuit of sexual conquest. For Tom, each new "target" represented not just sexual gratification, but a temporary fix for deeper feelings of inadequacy and shame that had roots in severe childhood neglect.

Tom's story illustrates something crucial: sex addiction isn't about being highly sexual or having poor moral character. Tom loved his wife deeply. He wanted desperately to be faithful. Yet despite devastating consequences, he couldn't stop acting-out, continuing his behaviors even in the face of serious behaviors despite serious negative consequences.

The Hidden Epidemic

Meet Dan, a 40-year-old married man and the father of two small children, all of whom he dearly loves. And yet he can't wait until they all go to sleep or go shopping or go to the playground, because then he can turn on his computer and steal whatever private moments that are available to access porn. He frantically searches through thousands of images, not really looking for anything specific but instead desperately trying shut out the many things he is constantly anxious about, like his ailing father, the precariousness of his job, the family's bills. He spends hours late at night, exhausting himself and undermining his ability to function well at the very job he is worried about losing. Dan has recently been warned by his boss that he doesn't seem "with it." He is disgusted with himself and takes it out on his children by being irritable or withdrawn from family activities. His wife worries about why he is no longer interested in being intimate with her, wondering if it is somehow her fault.

Dan represents what may be the most common form of sex addiction in our digital age. With pornography more accessible than ever before, millions of people like Dan find themselves trapped in compulsive viewing patterns that began innocently enough. Dan was first exposed to pornographic magazines in his early teens, but didn't start accessing online porn until five years ago, during a particularly stressful period at work. What was used initially for occasional "stress relief" quickly escalated into a daily necessity.

The progression was insidious. Dan began categorizing his life into "safe" times when he could use pornography and "dangerous" times when he might be discovered. He installed password-protected folders, learned to clear browser histories, and even created fake work projects to explain late nights at the computer. His tolerance grew. What once provided relief now required increasingly extreme or lengthy sessions to achieve the same numbing effect.

The impact on his neurobiology was profound. Chronic pornography use had dysregulated his dopamine system, making normal pleasures, like playing with his children, intimate moments with his wife, even work accomplishments feel flat and unrewarding by comparison. This phenomenon, known as tolerance, is identical to what happens with chemical addictions.

Dan's pornography use demonstrates another crucial aspect of sex addiction: it's primarily about emotional regulation rather than sexual gratification. Notice how Dan uses pornography to numb anxiety about his father's health, job security, and financial stress. The sexual content isn't the point. It's the temporary escape from overwhelming feelings that drives his compulsive behavior.

The Clinical Reality

These are just two examples of the many hundreds of individuals I have worked with over the past 30 years who fit the diagnosis of sex and/or porn addicts. All of them, including Tom and Dan, share the painful and destructive characteristics that are the hallmark of these addictions: Repeatedly engaging in sexual behavior (or obsessive sexual fantasy) despite the fact that there are serious adverse consequences in a major life area. Family life, professional status, reputation, physical health, financial security, relationship stability, and emotional and spiritual well-being all may be risked in the pursuit of a sexual high and the numbing it offers.

In sum, the sex and porn addict is someone who has lost control over his or her sexual behavior. Self-disgust, self-condemnation, shame, promises, attempts to exercise willpower, their best efforts at self-control, none of these have resulted in anything more than a temporary halt to the negative behaviors. For many individuals struggling with sex addiction like Tom and Dan, the path to treatment begins with a discovery: a partner finding evidence of hidden behaviors on a phone, computer, or credit card statement. This moment of revelation, while devastating for the partner, often becomes the catalyst that breaks through years of denial and secrecy.

- **The diagnostic criteria for sex addiction**

Although unfortunately not yet included in the DSM-5, the diagnostic criteria closely mirror those for substance use disorders:

- **Loss of Control:** The person cannot stop or limit their sexual behavior despite wanting to do so. They may set rules for themselves ("I'll only look at pornography on weekends") but consistently break these self-imposed boundaries.

- **Continued Use Despite Consequences:** The behavior continues even when it causes significant problems in relationships, work, finances, or health. They may lose jobs, marriages, or face legal consequences, yet the behavior persists.

- **Tolerance:** Over time, more extreme or frequent behaviors are needed to achieve the same effect. What once satisfied now feels inadequate to produce the dopamine response.

- **Withdrawal:** When unable to engage in the behavior, they experience irritability, anxiety, depression, or physical discomfort.

- **Preoccupation:** Much of their mental energy is consumed by thinking about, planning, or engaging in sexual behavior. This preoccupation interferes with daily functioning.

- **Escalation:** The behaviors often become more risky, frequent, or extreme over time, in response to the development of tolerance.

The Paradox of Motivation

What makes this particularly tragic is that these individuals often have tremendous motivation to stop. They hate what they're doing. They see the pain they're causing. They make sincere promises and genuine attempts at change. But addiction isn't about willpower or moral character; it's about brain chemistry, trauma responses, and learned coping mechanisms that require professional intervention to address effectively.

I've watched clients break down in my office as they describe the disconnect between their values and their actions. "I'm not this person," they say. "This isn't who I want to be." The cognitive dissonance is excruciating: they are simultaneously the person engaging in these behaviors and the person horrified by them.

The shame cycle becomes self-perpetuating. Sexual acting-out leads to shame, which leads to emotional pain, which leads to more sexual acting out to escape the pain. Each cycle deepens the neurological pathways that drive the addiction, making it progressively harder to break free through willpower and effort alone.

For some, drugs eventually enter the picture, and sometimes more extreme behaviors are added. Without appropriate, in-depth treatment the downward spiral will rapidly escalate. I've seen brilliant professionals lose careers, loving parents lose custody of their children, and devoted spouses lose marriages, all because they couldn't stop behaviors they desperately wanted to stop.

The progression can be frighteningly rapid. A client might start with occasional pornography use, escalate to paying for sex, then to increasingly risky encounters. Some develop fetishes or engage in behaviors they once found repugnant. Others accumulate massive debt from phone sex, webcam sex, escort services, or repeated trips to strip clubs and massage parlors. The common thread is the inability to stop despite mounting negative consequences.

The Deeper Truth

And yet, despite all this talk about sexual behavior and the label "sex" addict, we can also say that "Sex addiction is no more about sex than alcoholism is about thirst." This makes more sense when you examine the backgrounds of individuals who become sex addicts. Research has repeatedly shown that almost without exception, sex and porn addicts have suffered childhood abuse and neglect that has resulted in underlying and unresolved childhood trauma. Many also come from backgrounds where multi-addicted caregivers are unable to shelter them or attend to their needs, such as teaching them adequate coping skills when faced with discomfort or stress. For many sex addicts, sexual behavior early in life becomes the only means of self-soothing that is available to them.

The Adverse Childhood Experiences (ACE) scores of sex addicts are consistently higher than the general population. These experiences might include physical, sexual, or emotional abuse; neglect; household dysfunction such as domestic violence, substance abuse, or mental illness; or early exposure to sexual content or behavior. Each of these experiences can dysregulate the developing nervous system, creating a brain that struggles with emotional regulation, impulse control, and healthy attachment.

For many sex addicts, their early sexual experiences, whether consensual or not, become associated with emotional relief or comfort. This creates a powerful neurological association between sexual stimulation and emotional regulation that can be long-lasting. The brain essentially learns that sexual behavior equals emotional safety or numbness.

Like other addicts, the sex addict progressively establishes a pathological relationship with a mood changer: in this case, with an experience rather than a substance. The addiction cycle, emotional distress followed by sexual acting-out and fantasy, followed by shame and guilt, and then followed by more sex and/or fantasy to relieve the emotional distress that such feelings cause, takes the addict deeper and deeper into self-perpetuating negative behaviors. It is helpful to realize this when questioning why Tom or Dan didn't just stop their behaviors when they realized the painful consequences the behaviors were generating.

Understanding the Neurobiological Reality

Modern neuroscience has revealed that behavioral addictions create the same brain changes as chemical addictions. The prefrontal cortex, which is responsible for decision-making and impulse control, becomes compromised, while the limbic system's reward pathways become hypersensitive to addiction-related cues.

This means that for someone in active sex addiction, seeing a triggering image or being in a certain location can create an immediate neurochemical cascade that overwhelms rational decision-making. The person literally experiences a temporary hijacking of their conscious will. This isn't an excuse: it's a biological reality that informs effective treatment approaches.

The good news is that the brain's neuroplasticity means these changes can be reversed with appropriate treatment and time. Recovery literally rewires the brain, restoring healthy functioning to damaged neural pathways.

Beyond the Stereotypes

Sex addiction affects people across all demographics, men and women, young and old, religious and secular, married and single, gay and straight, wealthy and poor. While men are more likely to act out through pornography and prostitution, women are more likely to use romantic relationships, affairs, or fantasy to regulate their emotions or to buoy their self-esteem. Research shows, however, that while women's pornography consumption and sex addiction rates are lower than men's, they are still significant. The underlying addiction process is identical regardless of gender or specific behaviors.

For clinicians, partners, and family members, understanding that sex addiction is a genuine neurobiological condition, rooted in childhood trauma, not a moral failing or lack of willpower, is crucial for effective intervention and healing. This doesn't minimize the harm caused or excuse the behavior, but it provides a framework for understanding why traditional approaches like couples therapy or moral appeals often fail to create lasting change.

The path to recovery requires addressing both the addictive behaviors and the underlying trauma and emotional dysregulation that drive them. With proper treatment, people can and do recover from sex addiction, rebuilding their lives and relationships in ways they never thought possible. But first, they need to understand that what they're experiencing has a name, has a cause, and most importantly, has a path to recovery.

2. Isn't Sex Addiction Just Another Name for Promiscuity?

As noted above, sex addiction is no more about sex than alcoholism is about thirst. It is not defined by the nature of the sexual behaviors, the frequency of the behaviors, or the number of sexual partners. Although sex addicts may engage in sex with multiple partners, that is not a defining characteristic. Sex addicts may, for example, be primarily addicted to pornography and therefore engage mostly in solitary sexual behavior.

The reality is that sex addiction manifests in countless ways that have nothing to do with multiple partners. I've worked with clients whose addiction centered entirely on compulsive masturbation (sometimes 9 or 10 times a day), destroying their ability to function at work or maintain relationships. Others are consumed by fantasy addiction, spending 6 to 8 hours daily in elaborate imaginary sexual scenarios that prevent them from engaging with reality. Still others compulsively seek out prostitutes, massage parlors, or engage in exhibitionism or voyeurism. The behavior itself is less important than the compulsive, out-of-control nature of it.

Sex addiction can occur even within a monogamous relationship, when sex is used to numb painful feelings rather than to deepen a connection with a partner. I've treated married individuals who demand sex from their spouse multiple times a day not out of love or desire, but as a way to manage anxiety, anger, depression, or trauma responses. Their partners often describe feeling like objects rather than lovers, used for emotional regulation rather than genuine intimacy.

Sex addiction, in contrast to promiscuity, is not about chosen behaviors, but rather is something engaged in compulsively. The key diagnostic indicator is the continued engagement despite severe negative consequences. When someone loses jobs, relationships, financial stability, or legal standing but cannot stop the behavior, we're looking at addiction, not choice. I've met with clients who have destroyed their marriages, lost custody of their children, faced criminal charges, contracted STIs, and yet were still unable to stop. This is the hallmark of addiction: the complete loss of control despite devastating consequences.

Additionally, sex addiction fits the criteria for it to be classified as a disease, whereas promiscuity is often associated, rightly or wrongly, with immorality or looseness of character. Like other addictions, sex addiction involves changes in brain chemistry and neural pathways. Neuroimaging studies show that sex addicts have similar brain patterns to those with substance addictions, particularly in areas related to impulse control, decision-making, and reward processing. The addiction takes over the brain's reward system, making the compulsive behavior feel as necessary and urgent as food or water.

For the sex addict, sex is more about pain relief than it is about pleasure or true sexual desire. What initially starts as a problem-solver eventually become the problem. As the addiction progresses, clients describe their sexual behaviors as mechanical, joyless, and driven by an ever more urgent need to escape emotional pain. They're not pursuing pleasure; they're running from trauma, shame, anxiety, or depression. The sexual behavior provides temporary relief from psychological suffering, much like alcohol provides temporary relief for the alcoholic. This is why simply telling a sex addict to "just stop" is as ineffective as telling an alcoholic to "just stop drinking."

It's also crucial to understand that sex addiction often escalates over time. What begins as occasional pornography use or casual encounters frequently progresses to more frequent, risky, and extreme behaviors. I've seen clients move from mainstream pornography to increasingly violent content, from occasional affairs to repetitive use of prostitution, from mild exhibitionism to serious criminal behavior. This escalation pattern mirrors other addictions where tolerance builds and more intense experiences are needed to achieve the same relief.

That sex addiction is a disease is not to say that the sex addict shouldn't be held accountable for his or her behavior. All of the significant people surrounding the addict, from partners to children to employers to society at large, are negatively affected by those behaviors, even if they remain undetected for some period of time. Those painful, often destructive consequences must be addressed if the sex addict's recovery is to be complete, reparative, and transformative.

Understanding this distinction between addiction and promiscuity is essential for effective treatment. Moral judgments and shame-based interventions typically drive the addiction deeper underground, while a combination of addiction remediation and trauma-based treatment that addresses the underlying pain and childhood wounds can lead to genuine healing and behavioral change.

3. What's the Difference Between Someone Who is a Sex Addict and Someone Who Just Has a Normally High Sex Drive?

Healthy sexuality is grounded in desire and sexual appetite, and its goals generally include pleasure, emotional and physical satisfaction, and connection. Someone with a healthy sexual appetite is able to make decisions about when and with whom to be sexual. The sex addict, in contrast, compulsively engages in sexual behavior despite adverse consequences, and is driven by an attempt to reduce emotional pain. The outcome of such behavior is frequently negative feelings such as guilt, shame, and isolation rather than pleasure and satisfaction.

This distinction is absolutely critical for clinicians to understand, because the two can appear remarkably similar on the surface. I've had clients come to me convinced they're sex addicts simply because they want sex daily, or partners who assume their spouse is addicted because of a high libido. The frequency of sexual behavior is never the issue: it's the relationship to choice and consequence that matters.

Someone with a healthy high sex drive maintains agency over their sexual choices. They can choose not to be sexual when it's inappropriate (during work hours, for example, when their partner isn't interested, when they're in recovery from illness, or when it would jeopardize important relationships or responsibilities). They experience sexual desire as one appetite among many, not as an overwhelming compulsion that drowns out all other considerations.

The sex addict, by contrast, has lost this fundamental capacity for choice. I've worked with clients who've masturbated in workplace bathrooms despite knowing they could be fired for their repeated absences from their responsibilities, who've spent their children's college funds on prostitutes, who've had sex with strangers while their spouse battled cancer. These aren't choices driven by high libido; they're compulsions driven by an inability to tolerate emotional pain or anxiety without acting out sexually in an attempt to numb those feelings.

Here's a practical way to distinguish between the two: Explore the aftermath. Someone with a healthy high sex drive typically feels satisfied, connected, and energized after sexual activity. The sex addict almost invariably describes feeling worse afterward: ashamed, empty, disgusted, or anxious to repeat the behavior again soon. This is known as "borrowing tomorrow's peace of mind": sexual behavior that offers temporary relief but always comes with interest in the form of increased shame and compulsion.

Another key indicator is the ability to postpone sexual gratification. Someone with a healthy sex drive can delay sexual activity for appropriate reasons without significant distress. The sex addict experiences postponement as almost unbearable, like asking someone holding their breath to wait just a little longer before breathing. The urgency they feel is disproportionate to any reasonable sexual need.

The motivation is also fundamentally different. Healthy sexuality is approach-motivated: the individual is drawn toward pleasure, intimacy, and connection. Sex addiction is avoidance-motivated: the individual is running from emotional pain, trauma responses, anxiety, or depression. This is why addressing only the sexual behavior in treatment is insufficient. If you don't address what the person is running from, they'll simply find another way to run.

I've also observed that people with healthy high sex drives typically have sexual fantasies and behaviors that are relatively consistent over time. Sex addicts, however, often describe escalating patterns, needing more frequent, more intense, or more risky behaviors to achieve the same emotional numbing effect. What worked to manage their pain six months ago no longer provides sufficient relief, driving them toward increasingly extreme behaviors, sometimes including the use of drugs to potentiate the experience.

Frequency of sexual behavior should not be a determining factor in diagnosing sexual addiction. Repeated destructive consequences are. I've treated individuals who acted out sexually only once or twice a month, but each incident resulted in profound consequences: job loss, relationship destruction, legal problems, or serious health risks. Conversely, I've known people who have sex multiple times daily in the context of loving relationships with no negative impact on their lives or well-being.

The litmus test is always this: Can they stop when stopping is in their best interest? Someone with a healthy sex drive can choose celibacy during a partner's illness, can avoid sexual behavior that would jeopardize their marriage or career, and can moderate their sexual activity based on circumstances. The sex addict continues the behavior even when they desperately want to stop, even when they can clearly see it's destroying everything they value. This powerlessness over their behavior, combined with the continued engagement despite devastating consequences, is what distinguishes addiction from appetite.

4. From Behaviors to Impact: The Full Scope of Sexual Addiction

Understanding the Numbers

The actual prevalence of sexual addiction remains challenging to quantify precisely, due to the shame, secrecy, and lack of standardized diagnostic criteria surrounding this condition. However, the available data paints a concerning picture of both the scale of the problem and its far-reaching consequences.

Conservative estimates suggest that 10-12% of the population struggles with sexual addiction, though these figures may significantly underrepresent the actual scope. The sheer magnitude of the commercial sex industry provides compelling evidence that these numbers could be much higher. The pornography industry alone generates an estimated $100 billion annually, with consumption patterns that suggest widespread compulsive behavior rather than casual use.

The statistics on internet pornography consumption are particularly striking. Approximately 40 million people regularly visit pornographic websites, with women comprising one-third of this population, a figure that challenges outdated assumptions about who is affected by sexual addiction. The scale of engagement is staggering, with over 81 million pornography searches conducted daily. Research indicates that nearly 9% of those who access internet pornography develop addictive patterns of use.

Even within religious communities, where sexual restraint is often emphasized, the problem is pervasive. A recent survey found that 47% of Christians identified pornography as a major problem in their homes, highlighting how sexual addiction transcends cultural, religious, and social boundaries.

The Hidden Nature of the Problem

These statistics undoubtedly represent only the tip of the iceberg. Sexual addiction thrives in secrecy and shame, making accurate reporting extremely difficult. Many individuals never seek help, never disclose their struggles, and never appear in any statistical analysis. The stigma surrounding sexual problems means that both those directly affected and their families often suffer in silence, shame, or ignorance.

The data also reveals important demographic shifts. The traditional view of sexual addiction as primarily a male problem is being challenged by increasing recognition of female sex addiction. Women now represent a significant portion of those struggling with compulsive sexual behavior, though they may express it differently and face additional barriers to recognition and treatment.

The Workplace Impact of Sexual Addiction

The infiltration of compulsive sexual behavior into professional settings reveals the addiction's grip on daily functioning. While studies show that 30-45% of employees access pornography during work hours, most limit their usage to an average of 13 minutes. The sex addict, however, cannot exercise this restraint. Some may continue viewing pornographic content even when they know their internet usage is monitored and that accessing such material could result in termination.

This compulsive behavior demonstrates the hallmark of addiction: the inability to stop despite knowledge of serious consequences. The sex addict may repeatedly promise themselves they'll stop, may be fully aware of company policies, and may even fear losing their job, yet they struggle to control their behavior.

The Impact on Others

Sexual addiction is never an isolated problem. Each person struggling with sexual addiction is estimated to negatively impact at least five other people, including spouses, children, extended family members, friends, and colleagues. This multiplier effect means that the 10-12% prevalence rate actually touches the lives of a much larger percentage of the population.

The consequences extend across multiple domains of life. Marriages suffer from betrayal trauma, broken trust, and emotional disconnection. Children may experience neglect, exposure to inappropriate material, or the trauma of family dissolution. Financial stability can be threatened through spending on sex-related services, lost productivity, or job loss. Health risks multiply through potential exposure to sexually transmitted infections or the physical consequences of risky sexual behaviors.

Beyond Individual Suffering

The broader societal implications include increased healthcare costs, reduced workplace productivity, family breakdown, and the perpetuation of sex-related industries that may exploit vulnerable individuals. The economic impact alone, considering lost work productivity, increased healthcare utilization, legal costs, and family dissolution, likely reaches into the billions of dollars annually.

The Urgency of Recognition

The available statistics about the prevalence of sex addiction underscore the critical need for increased awareness, reduced stigma, and improved access to appropriate treatment. When a problem affects millions of individuals directly and impacts the lives of millions more, it can no longer be dismissed as a niche issue or moral failing. Sexual addiction represents a significant public health challenge that demands the same level of attention and resources devoted to other widespread addictive disorders.

The scope of sexual addiction's impact, from individual suffering to family destruction to workplace dysfunction, makes clear that this is not merely a personal problem but a societal issue requiring comprehensive response, understanding, and evidence-based treatment approaches.

Understanding the Scope of the Behaviors

The following is a comprehensive list of behaviors that sex addicts may engage in:

Important Notes:

- Not all of these behaviors by themselves constitute sexual addiction. The key factors are compulsivity, inability to stop despite negative consequences, and interference with life functioning

- Many of these behaviors can be engaged in healthy ways by non-addicts; addiction is characterized by loss of control and continued engagement despite negative consequences

- Some behaviors listed may be illegal and can have serious legal consequences

- The progression of sexual addiction often involves escalation from less risky to more risky behaviors over time

- Co-occurring mental health conditions or substance abuse can influence the types of behaviors exhibited

Compulsive Masturbation and Fantasy

- Excessive masturbation that interferes with daily functioning, work, or relationships, often based on pornography but also inspired by fantasy

- Compulsive consumption of pornography, including escalation to more extreme content

- Chronic sexual fantasy that dominates mental activity throughout the day

- Masturbation in inappropriate or risky locations (workplace, public restrooms, vehicles)

- Using masturbation as primary coping mechanism for stress, anxiety, or other emotions

- Inability to be sexually intimate with partner without fantasizing about others

Online Sexual Behaviors

- Compulsive viewing of internet pornography for hours at a time

- Engaging in cybersex or sexual chat rooms

- Live cam interactions with performers

- Sexting with multiple partners or strangers

- Creating fake online personas to engage in sexual conversations

- Compulsive use of dating apps purely for sexual encounters

- Viewing illegal sexual content

- Sharing or requesting explicit images compulsively

Extramarital Affairs and Multiple Partners

- Serial infidelity or ongoing affairs despite committed relationships

- One-night stands or casual sexual encounters with strangers
- Maintaining multiple simultaneous secret sexual relationships
- Emotional affairs that become sexualized
- Sex with acquaintances, coworkers, or friends' partners
- Seeking sex immediately after relationship conflicts

Commercial Sexual Services

- Frequent use of escort services or prostitutes
- Visiting massage parlors for sexual services
- Engaging with and financing "sugar babies" or maintaining other financial sexual arrangements
- Compulsive use of strip clubs beyond occasional visits
- Phone sex services or premium adult chat lines
- Sex tourism or traveling specifically to access commercial sex

Anonymous and Risky Sexual Encounters

- Cruising public places for anonymous sexual encounters (parks, restrooms, adult bookstores)
- Engaging in sex with strangers from online hookup sites
- Repeatedly participating in group sex or sex parties with unknown participants
- Having unprotected sex despite knowledge of risks

- Sexual encounters while under the influence of substances
- Sex in dangerous locations or situations with dangerous people

Exhibitionism and Voyeurism

- Exposing oneself sexually in public or semi-public places
- Flashing or exposing genitals to strangers
- Engaging in sexual activity in locations where discovery is likely
- Secretly watching others in sexual or intimate situations
- Taking unauthorized photos or videos of people in sexual contexts
- Compulsive sharing of one's own nude images

Sexual Harassment and Boundary Violations

- Making repeated unwanted sexual advances despite clear rejection
- Inappropriate touching or sexual comments in workplace or social settings
- Persistent sexual pursuit of unavailable individuals
- Sexual boundary violations with clients, students, or those in subordinate positions
- Groping or inappropriate touching in crowds or public transportation

- Making sexual comments or gestures that make others uncomfortable

Compulsive Dating and Seduction

- Serial dating with the primary goal of sexual conquest
- Love bombing or intense romantic pursuit followed by sexual abandonment
- Maintaining dating profiles while in committed relationships
- Compulsive flirting or seductive behavior in inappropriate settings
- Using emotional manipulation to obtain sexual encounters
- Targeting vulnerable individuals for sexual purposes

Phone and Technology-Based Behaviors

- Compulsive calling of phone sex lines
- Creating multiple social media accounts for sexual purposes
- Sending unsolicited explicit messages or images
- Hacking or stalking others' social media for sexual content
- Using hidden cameras or recording devices for sexual purposes
- Compulsive searching for sexual content on any available device

Workplace Sexual Behaviors

- Sexual relationships with subordinates or those in power-differential situations

- Viewing pornography where others might see it or engaging in sexual behaviors during work hours

- Making the workplace environment sexually charged through comments or behaviors

- Sexual harassment of coworkers

- Using work computer or resources for sexual purposes

- Sexual relationships that violate professional ethics or boundaries

Financial Sexual Behaviors

- Spending significant money on sexual services, pornography, or sexual encounters

- Financial arrangements for sex (sugar relationships, pay-per-meet arrangements)

- Compulsive spending on sex toys, pornography, or sexual paraphernalia

- Using household or business funds for sexual purposes without partner's knowledge

- Going into debt to finance sexual behaviors

- Stealing or appropriating money to pay for sexual services

Substance-Enhanced Sexual Behaviors

- Using drugs or alcohol specifically to facilitate sexual encounters
- Chemsex or party-and-play scenarios combining substance use with sex
- Seeking sexual encounters while intoxicated as a way to avoid emotional responsibility
- Using substances to lower inhibitions for risky sexual behaviors
- Combining sexual addiction with substance abuse in cyclical patterns

Compulsive Romantic Obsessions

- Serial intense crushes or obsessions with unavailable people
- Stalking behaviors focused on romantic or sexual targets
- Fantasy relationships with celebrities, coworkers, or acquaintances
- Emotional affairs that consume significant mental and emotional energy
- Love addiction patterns that quickly become sexualized

Sexual Behaviors with Power Dynamics

- Seeking sexual encounters where significant power and status differentials exist

- Sexual relationships with much younger or more vulnerable partners
- Using professional position to obtain sexual encounters
- Sexual behaviors that involve dominance, submission, or control as primary motivation
- Seeking sexual encounters with people in crisis or vulnerable situations

Ritualistic or Compulsive Sexual Patterns

- Following rigid routines or rituals around sexual behaviors
- Needing specific scenarios, locations, or circumstances to achieve sexual satisfaction
- Compulsive behaviors around sexual timing, frequency, or methodology
- Sexual behaviors tied to specific emotional states or life events
- Escalating sexual behaviors that become increasingly risky or extreme over time

Sexual Behaviors Outside Typical Orientation or Preferences

- **Compulsive sexual behaviors that cross typical orientation boundaries:** Sex addicts may engage in sexual behaviors with individuals who fall outside their usual sexual orientation or preferences. This often occurs as the addiction progresses and previous behaviors no longer provide the same level of stimulation or escape. For example, heterosexual men may compulsively seek sexual encounters with other men, or individuals may engage sexually with transgender persons despite this not aligning with their typical attractions. These behaviors are generally driven by the addictive process rather than authentic sexual orientation or preference. They represent the addiction's progression toward novelty, risk, or taboo experiences rather than genuine sexual identity exploration.

Similarly, individuals may engage in sexual activities, fetishes, or scenarios that they would normally find unappealing or even disturbing when not in the grip of addictive urges. The compulsive nature of the addiction can override typical preferences, boundaries, or values, leading to sexual behaviors that feel foreign to the person's authentic sexual self.

- **Important Clarifications**

These addiction-driven behaviors should not be confused with healthy sexual exploration, questioning of sexual identity, or natural evolution of sexual preferences. The key distinction is that addiction-driven behaviors typically involve compulsion, shame, and a sense of being "driven" to act in ways that feel inconsistent with one's authentic self. In contrast, healthy sexual exploration involves conscious choice, self-acceptance, and behaviors that feel aligned with personal growth and authentic desires.

It's also crucial to understand that engaging in these behaviors does not necessarily indicate confusion about sexual orientation or gender identity. Instead, they are likely symptoms of the addiction's progression and the brain's search for increasingly novel or risky experiences to achieve the same neurochemical response that earlier behaviors once provided

A Note of Hope and Perspective

This above list demonstrates the wide range of sexual behaviors that can become compulsive and destructive when driven by addiction rather than healthy sexual expression, and it may feel overwhelming, frightening, or even shocking to read. Partners discovering their loved one's addiction, sex addicts recognizing their own patterns, students learning about this condition, or therapists new to this field might feel discouraged by the extensive range and severity of these behaviors. It's important to understand that no single individual engages in all or even most of these behaviors, and many people struggling with sexual addiction may identify with only a small subset of this list.

The purpose of presenting such a thorough catalog is not to alarm or discourage, but to provide complete information that validates the experiences of those affected and helps normalize the wide spectrum of behaviors that can fall under sexual addiction. For many people, seeing their specific struggles listed and recognized can provide immense relief: they are not alone, they are not uniquely broken, and their experiences are understood by professionals who specialize in this field.

More importantly, every behavior on this list represents something that can be addressed, healed, and overcome through proper treatment and recovery work. Sexual addiction, regardless of how severe or extensive the acting-out behaviors have become, is a treatable condition. Many thousands of individuals have found freedom from these compulsive patterns and have gone on to build healthy, fulfilling lives and relationships.

The powerfulness of sexual addiction—its ability to drive people to behaviors they never imagined they would engage in—is matched by the powerfulness of recovery when individuals commit to the healing process. While the list of behaviors may seem daunting, following sections of this guide outline proven pathways to recovery that have helped countless individuals reclaim their lives from this addiction.

Recovery is possible. Healing is available. Hope is real.

5. Breaking the Gender Myth: Sexual Addiction Affects Both Men and Women

One of the most persistent and harmful misconceptions about sexual addiction is that it primarily or exclusively affects men. This gender stereotype not only misrepresents the reality of sexual addiction but also creates additional barriers to recognition, diagnosis, and treatment for women who struggle with compulsive sexual behavior.

The Reality of Gender and Sexual Addiction

Sexual addiction affects both men and women, though the manifestations and social responses may differ significantly. The underlying neurobiological mechanisms of addiction, involving dopamine pathways, reward systems, and compulsive behavior patterns, operate similarly regardless of gender. The core diagnostic criteria for sexual addiction, including loss of control, continued behavior despite negative consequences, repeated efforts to stop the behaviors, and preoccupation with sexual thoughts and activities, apply equally to both men and women.

Shared Risk Factors Across Genders

The root causes and risk factors for sexual addiction show no gender preference. Childhood trauma and abuse, which are among the strongest predictors of later addiction behaviors, affect both boys and girls. Family histories of addiction, whether to substances, sex, or other behaviors, create vulnerability in children of all genders in two key ways. First, addiction has a genetic component that can be inherited regardless of gender, as decades of research has shown. Second, children growing up in addictive family systems often learn unhealthy coping mechanisms by watching their parents use addictive behaviors to manage stress, emotions, or problems instead of modeling healthy problem-solving skills.

When children don't learn effective ways to handle life's challenges, they become vulnerable to developing their own addictive patterns, often starting in childhood. This is where inadequate coping skills become a critical risk factor. Life inevitably brings stressors: work pressure, relationship conflicts, financial worries, health concerns, or major life transitions. Everyone experiences difficult emotions like anxiety, depression, loneliness, anger, or grief at various times.

People with healthy coping skills might handle these challenges through exercise, talking with friends, seeking professional help, engaging in hobbies, listening to music, or using relaxation techniques. However, those who never learned healthy strategies such as these instead turn to behaviors that provide immediate relief or escape, including compulsive sexual behavior. Sexual activity for both men and women can temporarily numb emotional pain or anxiety, provide a rush of pleasurable brain chemicals, or offer a distraction from overwhelming problems. But for those individuals who have developed increasing reliance on the temporary relief that sexual behavior offers, the very behavior that once brought relief eventually becomes a source of greater pain.

The Double Burden for Women

While the addiction itself may be similar across genders, women face unique challenges that can make their experience particularly difficult. Female sex addicts often carry an intensified burden of shame and guilt because their behavior conflicts so dramatically with societal expectations and norms for women's sexuality.

Societal gender roles have long positioned women as sexually passive, relationship-focused, and naturally monogamous. When a woman's sexual behavior becomes compulsive and potentially involves multiple partners, pornography use, or other activities outside these narrow expectations, she may experience profound shame about violating gender norms in addition to the shame inherent in addictive behavior.

This amplified shame creates several barriers to recovery. Women may be less likely to recognize their behavior as addiction, more likely to minimize or rationalize their actions, and significantly more reluctant to seek help. The fear of being labeled or judged as promiscuous, immoral, or mentally unstable can prevent women from accessing the support they desperately need.

Different Expressions, Same Addiction

While some female sex addicts do engage in behaviors similar to their male counterparts, including multiple sexual partners, frequenting sex-oriented establishments, or engaging with sex workers, many women's addictive sexual behavior takes different forms that may be less visible or recognized.

A significant portion of female sex addicts confine their acting out to internet-based sexual behaviors. This includes compulsive consumption of pornography, participation in sexual chat rooms, engagement in cybersex relationships, creation and sharing of exhibitionistic sexual content, and compulsive use of dating apps or websites for sexual validation rather than genuine connection.

The Appeal of Cyber-Based Acting Out for Women

The internet provides several advantages that make it particularly appealing to women struggling with sexual addiction. The anonymity offered by online platforms allows women to explore sexual behaviors without the immediate social consequences they might face in person. They can create alternate personas, engage in sexual conversations or activities, and maintain a degree of separation from their "real" identity.

The relative safety of cybersex also appeals to many women. Online sexual behavior eliminates many of the physical risks such as violence, sexually transmitted infections, or unwanted pregnancy associated with meeting unknown partners. Women can engage in sexually addictive behavior from the perceived safety of their homes while maintaining some control over the level of physical risk.

However, this perceived safety is often illusory. Online sexual behavior carries its own risks, including potential exposure or blackmail, financial exploitation, emotional manipulation, and the gradual escalation that may eventually lead to in-person encounters despite initial intentions to keep behavior confined to cyberspace.

Unique Presentations in Women

Female sexual addiction may also manifest in ways that don't fit traditional stereotypes. Some women become addicted to the validation and attention they receive through sexual behavior rather than the physical acts themselves. This might involve compulsive posting of provocative images on social media, engaging in emotional affairs, or constantly seeking sexual attention and validation from multiple sources.

Other women may express their sexual addiction through compulsive romantic relationships, serial monogamy where they move quickly from one intense sexual relationship to another, or through combinations of online and offline behaviors that create complex patterns of acting out. For some female sex addicts, professional sex work may be a means of expressing and satisfying their compulsive sexual behaviors.

Treatment Implications

Recognition that sexual addiction affects both genders has

important implications for treatment approaches that work for both sexes. Women, for example, may benefit from gender-specific therapy groups where they can address the unique shame and social pressures they face. Additionally, 12-Step sex addiction groups could support the formation of women-only groups, as recovering women might not feel comfortable in recovery groups comprised primarily of male sex addicts. Treatment programs also need to be sensitive to the different ways sexual addiction may manifest in women and avoid assumptions based on male-centered models of the disorder. Additionally, partners and family members of female sex addicts may need specialized support, as they may be dealing with their own confusion about how to understand and respond to behavior that challenges their expectations about women's sexuality. Society often portrays women as less sexually driven than men, so partners may struggle to understand how their wife or girlfriend could be acting out sexually with multiple partners or engaging in compulsive sexual behaviors. Family members may have particular difficulty accepting that women can be sexually aggressive, seek out anonymous encounters, or prioritize sexual acting-out over family responsibilities.

These cultural assumptions can lead to additional shame for the female addict and delayed recognition of the problem, as both the woman and her loved ones may dismiss early warning signs because the behaviors don't fit stereotypical expectations of how women "should" behave sexually. Partners may also face unique challenges in finding support groups or resources, as most materials and support networks have been designed with male addicts in mind..

The Importance of Breaking Gender Stereotypes

Recognizing sexual addiction as a disorder that affects both men and women is crucial for several reasons. It ensures that women receive appropriate diagnosis and treatment, reduces the shame and isolation that prevents many women from seeking help, and promotes a more accurate understanding of the nature of sexual addiction itself.

Breaking down gender stereotypes also helps families, partners, and healthcare providers recognize warning signs and respond appropriately regardless of the gender of the person affected. When sexual addiction is viewed as primarily a male problem, women's symptoms may be overlooked, minimized, or misdiagnosed, leading to prolonged suffering and delayed intervention.

The reality is that sexual addiction, like other forms of addiction, does not discriminate based on gender. Both men and women can develop compulsive sexual behaviors, both suffer from the consequences, and both deserve understanding, support, and appropriate treatment to recover from this challenging disorder.

6. What Are the Signs and Symptoms to Look for in a Person Who Is a Sex Addict?

Because the sex addict lives a secret life, it may be difficult to identify sexual addiction in a significant other or a co-worker. The secretive nature of this condition means that warning signs often emerge gradually and may initially be dismissed as personality quirks, stress responses, or temporary behavioral changes. Although none of the following signs and symptoms is a definitive diagnostic factor, a constellation of these factors may suggest the presence of an active sexual addiction, either in the home or at work.

Behavioral and Social Warning Signs

- **Constant use of sexual humor:** While occasional sexual humor is normal, sex addicts often rely on it excessively as a way to introduce sexual themes into conversations or to test boundaries with others. This humor may be inappropriate for the setting, persistent despite social cues to stop, or used as a deflection mechanism when feeling uncomfortable or anxious.

- **Sexualization of nonsexual situations (known as intriguing):** The individual consistently interprets neutral interactions, comments, or situations through a sexual lens. This might manifest as reading sexual intent into friendly gestures, turning mundane conversations toward sexual topics, or viewing colleagues, service providers, or acquaintances primarily as potential sexual partners rather than as whole people. The sex addict doesn't necessarily act on the sexual interaction; the intriguing itself provides the sought-for emotional hit.

- **Many short-term relationships:** A pattern of brief, intense romantic or sexual relationships that end abruptly, often without clear explanation. These relationships may be characterized by rapid sexual intimacy followed by emotional withdrawal, or the person may maintain multiple simultaneous relationships without disclosure to any of the partners.

- **Sexual boundary-crossing (sexual harassment):** This can range from subtle violations like inappropriate touching, sexual comments, or persistent advances despite clear rejection, to more overt harassment. In workplace settings, this might include making sexual comments about colleagues, sharing inappropriate content, or using position or authority to pursue sexual encounters. Not all sexual harassment can be attributed to sexual addiction, but repeated perpetration despite serious negative consequences suggests it may be a contributing factor in some cases.

- **Inappropriate or "accidentally" revealing dress:** Consistently choosing clothing that draws sexual attention, particularly in professional or family settings where such dress is inappropriate. The person may claim these choices are accidental or blame others for "sexualizing" their appearance while continuing the pattern.

Relationship and Emotional Indicators

- **Mood changes related to sexual behavior:** Noticeable shifts in mood, energy, or demeanor that correlate with sexual activity or opportunity. The person may become irritable, anxious, or depressed when sexual outlets are unavailable, or show dramatic mood improvements after sexual encounters. These mood swings often seem disproportionate to other life circumstances.

- **Diminished sexual interest in a partnership:** A hallmark of sexual addiction is the difficulty the addict has in combining sexuality and intimacy. Many sex addicts find themselves capable of intense sexual encounters with strangers or through pornography, but struggle to be sexually present with partners they truly love and care about. Their sexual relationships with intimate partners may become mechanical, infrequent, or entirely absent, even while they maintain compulsive sexual activity outside the relationship. This creates profound confusion and pain for partners, who may feel rejected and inadequate while unknowingly competing with the addict's secret sexual outlets. The addict's ability to be sexually active elsewhere while being sexually unavailable at home often makes partners question their own attractiveness and desirability, not understanding that the issue lies in the addict's inability to integrate authentic emotional connection with sexual expression.

- **Confusion of affection and sexuality:** The person may struggle to distinguish between emotional intimacy and sexual attraction, leading to attempts to sexualize friendships or misinterpreting caring gestures as sexual invitations. They may also have difficulty expressing or receiving non-sexual affection without it attempting to turn it into a sexual experience.

- **Emotional and sexual distance and a sense of unavailability:** Even when physically present, the person seems emotionally withdrawn or preoccupied. Partners often describe feeling like they're competing with something unknown for the person's attention and emotional availability. Preoccupation with planning for the next sexual experience or reminiscing about the last is common. Sexual fantasy is a major component of sexual addiction. The person may seem to be "somewhere else" mentally during conversations or intimate moments, or may become irritable when their fantasies or planning time is interrupted. Attempts at genuine emotional connection often feel forced or superficial.

- **Use of sexuality as a problem-solver:** The individual consistently turns to sexual experiences or fantasy to cope with stress, anxiety, depression, anger, or other difficult emotions. Sex becomes their primary coping mechanism rather than one of many healthy strategies for managing life's stresses or challenges.

- **Patterns of lying, deception, and gaslighting:** Sex addicts typically develop elaborate systems of dishonesty to conceal their acting-out behaviors from partners and family members. This goes far beyond occasional white lies and becomes a pervasive pattern of deception that may include creating false alibis, maintaining secret email accounts or phones, deleting browser histories, and constructing detailed cover stories for unexplained absences. When confronted with evidence or suspicions, they often resort to gaslighting tactics, making their partner question their own perceptions, memory, or sanity.

    Common gaslighting behaviors include adamantly denying obvious evidence, claiming the partner is "paranoid" or "crazy," shifting blame onto the partner for being "controlling" or "suspicious," or minimizing discovered behaviors as "not that big a deal." This systematic dishonesty becomes a secondary addiction in itself, as the person becomes increasingly skilled at manipulation and may lie reflexively even about non-sexual matters. The deception often causes as much relationship damage as the sexual behaviors themselves, creating a profound erosion of trust that persists long into recovery.

Social and Professional Changes

- **Lack of participation in previously enjoyed familial or social events:** Gradual withdrawal from family gatherings, social activities, hobbies, or community involvement that were once important to the person. This withdrawal often occurs as the addiction consumes more time and mental energy, or as the person seeks to avoid situations where their behavior might be questioned.

- **Unexplained absences and lateness, at work and at home:** Frequent disappearances without satisfactory explanations, chronic tardiness, or extended breaks that can't be accounted for. The person may offer vague, inconsistent explanations or actual lies about their whereabouts, becoming defensive when questioned about their time. As noted above, gaslighting is a major defense against being challenged or discovered.

Physical, Emotional, and Financial Consequences

- **Inexplicable financial problems:** Money disappearing from accounts designated for retirement, savings, or children's college funds, as well as unexplained credit card charges, unpaid bills and financial strain that doesn't match the person's income or known expenses. This might include payments for online content, escort services, "sugar daddy commitments, frequent dating expenses, or costs associated with maintaining multiple relationships.

- **Repetitive health concerns:** Frequent visits to healthcare providers for sexually transmitted infection testing, recurring infections, or other health issues related to sexual activity. The person may show excessive anxiety about STIs or seek testing far more frequently than medically necessary.

- **Depression and anxiety:** Persistent feelings of sadness, hopelessness, shame, or worthlessness that may stem from the conflict between the person's values and their compulsive sexual behavior. This depression often coexists with anxiety, which also may worsen as the addiction progresses and negative consequences start to pile up.

The Progressive Nature of Sexual Addiction

Over time, as with all addictions, tolerance develops so that the need for new and different stimuli develops. What once provided satisfaction or relief no longer suffices, leading to an escalating pattern of behavior. This escalation may mean that riskier behaviors may occur, such as public sexual activity, unprotected sex with multiple partners, or engaging with increasingly dangerous individuals or situations.

Drugs or alcohol may be added in order to potentiate the sexual high, reduce inhibitions, or numb the shame and guilt associated with the behavior. This can lead to dangerous combinations of risk-taking that compound the potential for physical harm, legal consequences, or exposure of the secret life.

More time and money may be spent in pursuit of the sexual high, as the individual requires more frequent or intense experiences to achieve the same level of satisfaction or relief. Work performance may suffer as more time is devoted to seeking sexual encounters, viewing pornography, or engaging in sexual fantasy.

Relationships deteriorate as the person becomes less emotionally available and more deceptive about their activities.

The Point of Revelation

Sexual behavior and sexual fantasy are now becoming the central organizing principle of the individual's life, so that ordinary life activities and daily responsibilities are increasingly neglected. Career advancement, family relationships, financial stability, and personal health take a backseat to the pursuit of sexual experiences. The person's mental energy becomes consumed with planning, seeking, engaging in, and recovering from sexual encounters.

It is at this point that the addiction may be revealed, either through some sort of slip up that makes the situation obvious to a partner or employer, such as discovery of evidence on digital devices, being caught in compromising situations, facing legal consequences, or experiencing a serious health crisis, or sometimes through self-revelation because the addict has "hit bottom" and can no longer tolerate living a double life.

The revelation often comes as a shock to family members, friends, and colleagues who may have noticed individual warning signs but didn't recognize the full scope of the problem. The secret nature of sexual addiction means that even those closest to the individual may have been completely unaware of the extent of the compulsive behavior.

Important Considerations

It's crucial to remember that the presence of some of these signs doesn't automatically indicate sexual addiction. Many of these behaviors can result from other mental health conditions, life stressors, relationship problems, or medical issues. Additionally, cultural factors, personal values, and individual differences in sexual expression must be considered when evaluating these potential warning signs.

Professional assessment by a qualified mental health provider with expertise in sexual addiction is essential for accurate diagnosis and appropriate treatment planning. The complexity of this condition requires careful evaluation to distinguish between sexual addiction and other conditions that may present with similar symptoms.

7. What About the Spouses and Partners of Sex Addicts? What Is Their Story?

Before a sexual addiction surfaces for full acknowledgment, those closely involved with a sex addict may be oblivious to the presence of the problem or may have only a vague sense that something is amiss in the relationship. Partners often describe living with a persistent feeling that "something isn't right" but struggle to identify what's wrong. They may notice emotional distance, unexplained mood changes, defensive reactions to innocent questions, or a general sense of their partner being unavailable even when physically present.

Although an important diagnostic factor in sexual addiction is difficulty in combining intimacy and sexuality in a relationship (either intimacy is present while sexuality is not or sexuality is present while intimacy is not), partners of sex addicts may tolerate an inadequate or incomplete relationship because they too have difficulty in experiencing relationships of that depth. This tolerance often stems from their own attachment wounds or family-of-origin issues that make incomplete intimacy feel familiar or normal.

Studies have shown that sex addicts and their partners have very similar childhood histories, often including emotional neglect, inconsistent caregiving, trauma, or family dysfunction. This shared background can create an unconscious attraction between individuals who are comfortable with similar levels of emotional unavailability. Partners may have developed their own coping mechanisms, such as people-pleasing, hypervigilance, detachment, or emotional self-sufficiency, that actually enable the addictive system to continue undetected. For instance, a codependent or compliant partner might consistently excuse their spouse's unexplained absences or mood swings, telling themselves "he's under a lot of stress at work" rather than questioning the behavior directly. They may take on increasing household or familial responsibilities without complaint, essentially covering for their and partner's emotional unavailability and allowing them more freedom to pursue addictive behaviors.

Hypervigilant partners often become experts at reading their spouse's moods and anticipating their needs, walking on eggshells to avoid conflict that might reveal uncomfortable truths. They may obsessively monitor bank statements or phone records but then dismiss red flags they discover, convincing themselves there must be innocent explanations rather than confronting the evidence.

Partners who cope through emotional detachment might intellectualize problems in the relationship, focusing on practical matters while avoiding deeper emotional connection. This detachment can provide the addict with relief from intimacy demands while maintaining the appearance of a functional relationship. Meanwhile, emotionally self-sufficient partners pride themselves on "not being needy," rarely expressing their own wants or concerns. They may say things like "I don't need much" or "I can handle things myself," which inadvertently gives the addict permission to remain emotionally unavailable and continue investing their energy elsewhere.

These adaptive strategies, while originally developed for emotional survival, can inadvertently create an environment where the addiction remains hidden and the addict faces fewer natural consequences for their behavior.

The Impact of Discovery: Betrayal Trauma

When sexual addiction is discovered or disclosed, partners experience what is characterized as betrayal trauma. This is not simply disappointment or anger about infidelity; it's a complex psychological injury that results from the shattering of fundamental assumptions about reality, safety, who their partner is, and the relationship itself. The systematic deception that typically accompanies sexual addiction means partners have been living in a false reality, often for years.

For the spouse or partner, shock, deep feelings of betrayal, confusion, and anger are common initial responses. They feel like their reality has been completed upended. Many partners describe feeling like they're "going crazy" as they try to reconcile the person they thought they knew with the reality of the person who has maintained this addiction. The discovery often triggers a flood of memories as partners reinterpret past events through the lens of this new information. Unexplained behaviors, financial discrepancies, or emotional distance suddenly make devastating sense.

For many, Post-Traumatic Stress Disorder symptoms may result, including intrusive thoughts, hypervigilance, sleep disturbances, anxiety attacks, and emotional numbing. These symptoms require professional support and both individual and group treatment to work through those painful feelings and to help the partner decide if he or she wishes to participate in the ongoing work of trying to regain emotional trust and heal the relationship.

The Partner's Recovery Process

Partners need their own recovery program that focuses on healing from betrayal trauma rather than simply learning to cope with their partner's addiction. This process typically involves:

- **Processing the trauma of discovery and deception:** The discovery of sexual addiction creates a unique form of trauma that combines the shock of betrayal with the disorientation of realizing that one's perceived and trusted reality was false. Partners often experience symptoms similar to those seen in other trauma survivors: intrusive memories of discovering evidence, nightmares, panic attacks, and an inability to trust their own perceptions. Processing this trauma involves working through intense emotions like rage, grief, and profound sadness while learning to understand that their reactions are normal responses to an abnormal situation.

Many partners benefit from trauma-focused therapy approaches such as EMDR (Eye Movement Desensitization and Reprocessing), expressive experiential modalities such as psychodrama, and somatic therapies that help the body release stored trauma responses. This phase often includes grieving not just the relationship they thought they had, but also the person they believed their partner to be.

- **Rebuilding their sense of reality and self-trust:** Years of gaslighting and systematic deception can leave partners questioning their ability to perceive situations accurately. They may have been told they were "paranoid," "overly suspicious," or "crazy" when their intuition was actually detecting real problems. Rebuilding self-trust involves learning to validate their own experiences and perceptions again. This might include journaling to track patterns they notice to help them validate their perceptions, practicing mindfulness to reconnect with their intuitive responses, and working with a therapist to distinguish between trauma-based hypervigilance and healthy awareness. Partners often need to relearn how to trust their gut feelings about people and situations, as their partnership with an addict may have taught them to override their natural warning systems.

- **Addressing their own family-of-origin issues that may have contributed to accepting an inadequate relationship:** Many partners discover that their tolerance for emotional unavailability, inconsistency, or deception stems from childhood experiences that normalized these patterns. This might include growing up with an addicted parent, experiencing emotional neglect, witnessing domestic violence, or learning that love requires sacrifice of one's own needs. Recovery involves identifying these patterns, understanding how they developed as survival mechanisms, and consciously choosing new ways of relating. For example, a partner who learned as a child that questioning adults led to punishment may need to practice asking direct questions and setting boundaries, even when it feels frightening. Therapy often explores themes like "What did I learn about love in my family?" and "How did I learn to get my needs met?"

- **Learning healthy boundaries and communication skills:** Many partners have never learned to identify their own needs, much less communicate them effectively. Boundary-setting might involve learning to say "I'm not comfortable with that" without extensive justification, or "I need time to think about this" instead of immediately accommodating their partner's requests. Communication skills include learning to express feelings with "I statements" rather than using the blaming language of "You this or you that," asking for what they need directly, and listening to their partner's responses without automatically taking responsibility for their emotions. This often involves unlearning codependent communication patterns such as mind-reading ("I know what he meant"), caretaking ("Let me fix this for you"), or acquiescence ("If it makes you happy"). Partners may practice these skills in support groups or individual therapy before applying them in their primary relationship.

- **Deciding whether to stay in or leave the relationship based on their authentic needs rather than fear or codependency:** This decision-making process requires partners to differentiate between choices driven by fear (such as fear of being alone, financial insecurity, or concern about children) and choices aligned with their genuine values and desires. Partners often benefit from exploring questions like: "If I knew I would be okay either way, what would I choose?" "What kind of relationship do I actually want?" and "Am I staying because I love this person and believe we can build something healthy together, or because I'm afraid of the alternative?"

This process may involve practical planning (such as understanding their financial options), emotional work (grieving the loss of their envisioned future), and spiritual exploration (clarifying their values about marriage, forgiveness, and personal growth). Some partners choose to stay and work on the relationship, others decide to leave, and still others choose to take time in separation while both partners work on their individual recovery before making a final decision.

Both members of the couple need to become involved in a comprehensive recovery process if the relationship is to survive the discovery of a sexual addiction. However, the partner's recovery must be independent of the addict's progress. Many partners benefit from individual therapy, support groups specifically for partners of sex addicts, and couples therapy once both individuals have established some stability in their individual recovery processes.

The Possibility of Rebuilding Trust and Intimacy

Reestablishment of trust is often a long-term project requiring consistent, transparent behavior from the recovering addict and significant emotional work from both partners. Trust rebuilding involves not just the absence of acting-out behaviors, but the presence of emotional availability, honest communication, and genuine intimacy that may never have existed in the relationship before.

If the relationship is one that is based in love and both partners are committed to their individual recovery work, a successful but vastly changed intimate partnership can emerge. Many couples report that while the discovery of sexual addiction was devastating, the recovery process ultimately led them to a deeper, more authentic relationship than they had ever experienced. However, this outcome requires sustained commitment, professional support, and often years of dedicated work from both partners.

It's important to note that not all relationships survive sexual addiction, and choosing to end the relationship can also be a healthy outcome, particularly when the addict is unwilling to engage in genuine recovery or when the partner determines that rebuilding trust isn't possible or desirable for them.

8. Is There Treatment for Sexual Addiction?

Hope and Healing: What Recovery Requires

Recovery from sexual addiction is absolutely possible, and many thousands of individuals have found freedom from this condition. However, it's crucial to understand that healing from sex addiction is typically a long-term process that requires sustained commitment, professional support, and treatment that addresses the deep-seated trauma and attachment wounds that for many, if not all, addicts were experienced in childhood.

Recovery is not a quick fix or a simple matter of behavior modification, but rather a comprehensive transformation that addresses the whole person, their history as well as their current behaviors. The journey requires courage, patience, and willingness to do difficult emotional work, but it is fundamentally a process of healing that leads from despair to genuine hope. The result, a transformed life of authentic connection, emotional freedom, and integrated sexuality, makes the effort profoundly worthwhile.

The First Contact: Strong Motivation for Treatment

Motivation to engage in treatment is generally strong among those suffering from sexual addiction, primarily because they have been living an unmanageable life in which sex and fantasy have long since ceased to provide pleasure. What often had begun as pleasurable sexual experiences gradually became compulsive behavior driven by emotional pain, anxiety, depression, or trauma rather than genuine desire or healthy sexual appetite.

Many describe feeling trapped in a cycle where they feel compelled to act out sexually even when they derive no satisfaction or pleasure from it, often feeling disgusted, empty, or deeply ashamed immediately afterward. The behaviors that once offered escape, excitement, or temporary relief have transformed into sources of increasing despair and self-loathing. Instead of providing the emotional regulation or connection they desperately seek, these behaviors become repetitive attempts to fill an unfillable void, leaving them feeling more isolated and distressed than before.

For many, the recognition that their sexual behavior has become a source of suffering rather than satisfaction creates the crisis that finally motivates them to seek help. For some addicts, this level of dissatisfaction may lead them to unconsciously sabotage their own secrecy, making a mistake that ensures discovery and compels them to seek help.

The Relief of Recognition and Diagnosis

For many sex addicts, receiving a correct diagnosis of their problem and learning that they are not alone in their struggles provides enormous relief. For years, many, heeding societal messages, have felt like moral failures, believing they simply lack willpower or are fundamentally flawed as human beings. They may have tried repeatedly to stop their behaviors through sheer determination, religious commitment, or promises to partners, only to find themselves acting-out again despite their best intentions.

The shame and isolation that have characterized their experience begin to lift when they realize they have a recognized condition with established treatment approaches, and that many thousands of others have walked this path to recovery before them. This recognition marks a crucial turning point from self-condemnation to hope.

Understanding the Neurobiological Foundation

Learning that sexual addiction is a recognized condition with neurobiological underpinnings helps shift both addicts and their loved ones from shame-based self-condemnation to understanding that this is a treatable medical condition. Research has demonstrated that addiction fundamentally changes brain chemistry and neural pathways, particularly in areas related to reward, motivation, and impulse control.

The neurobiological vulnerability often begins much earlier than the addictive sexual behaviors themselves. Childhood trauma and neglect literally reshape the developing brain, particularly in areas governing emotional regulation, stress response, and attachment capacity. Children who experience trauma often develop dysregulated stress systems and impaired ability to self-soothe, creating a brain that becomes primed to seek external sources of relief and regulation. This early neurobiological foundation, characterized by hyperactive stress responses, underdeveloped impulse control centers, and disrupted attachment neurocircuitry, creates the soil in which sexual addiction can later take root.

When someone with this underlying neurobiological vulnerability encounters sexual stimulation, the brain's reward system becomes hijacked more readily than it might in someone without such early conditioning. This reward system, originally designed to reinforce behaviors necessary for survival, becomes co-opted by addictive behaviors, creating powerful cravings and compulsions that override rational decision-making. In sexual addiction, repeated engagement in compulsive sexual behaviors creates changes in the brain's dopamine pathways similar to those observed in substance addictions.

Over time, the brain begins to require increasingly intense or frequent sexual stimulation to achieve the same neurochemical response, leading to escalation and progressive loss of control. Additionally, the prefrontal cortex, the brain region responsible for decision-making, impulse control, and considering consequences, becomes increasingly impaired, making it genuinely difficult for addicts to "just stop" despite their sincere desire to do so. This creates a compounding effect where each episode of acting-out further strengthens the addictive pathways while often re-traumatizing the person through shame and consequences. This then drives even more compulsive behaviors seeking soothing.

Hope Through Understanding

Understanding these layered neurobiological realities helps both addicts and their loved ones recognize that addiction is not simply a matter of weak willpower or moral failing, but a complex condition that affects brain functioning at fundamental levels, often rooted in early developmental experiences beyond the person's control. This knowledge provides genuine hope because it demonstrates that with proper treatment addressing both the underlying trauma and the addictive patterns, along with sustained recovery efforts, the brain can heal and form new, healthier neural pathways.

Just as the brain learned both traumatic coping patterns and addictive behaviors through repetition and reinforcement, it can also learn recovery patterns through consistent practice of healthy behaviors (mindfulness, exercise, and honest communication, for example), along with trauma healing work and emotional regulation skills. This scientific understanding removes much of the shame and self-blame that keeps people trapped in addictive cycles, replacing it with compassionate recognition that healing is possible through comprehensive treatment that addresses both the roots and the branches of the addiction tree.

The Foundation: Self-Honesty

Before any meaningful recovery can begin, sex addicts need to develop a deep commitment to self-honesty (sometimes referred to as radical honesty), first with themselves, then with their therapists, sponsors, support groups, and ultimately with their partners. Years of living a double life, maintaining elaborate deception systems, and lying reflexively have created deeply ingrained patterns of dishonesty that extend far beyond covering up sexual behaviors.

This commitment to honesty represents a fundamental shift in how addicts relates to themselves and others. It means acknowledging the full extent of their behaviors without minimization or justification, recognizing the impact of their actions on others, and accepting responsibility for the harm they've caused. For many addicts, this level of honesty initially feels extremely frightening, as they've used deception as their primary method of emotional protection and control. However, as they experience being accepted and not abandoned despite their honesty, many discover profound relief in no longer carrying the burden of secrets and lies and the freedom that comes from authentic self-expression.

Developing self-honesty involves learning to identify and acknowledge feelings, needs, and motivations that have been buried under layers of shame, numbing, and denial. It means facing uncomfortable truths about their behavior patterns, the progression of their addiction, and the ways they've manipulated situations and people. This process often requires significant support from therapists, 12-Step sponsors, and recovery groups, as the tendency to revert to old patterns of deception can be strong, particularly when feeling ashamed or threatened.

The Therapeutic Relationship as Healing

The therapeutic relationship itself becomes a laboratory for learning healthy intimacy and attachment. Many sex addicts have never experienced a safe, boundaried relationship with appropriate emotional closeness, making the therapy relationship an important corrective emotional experience. Through this work, addicts learn to tolerate emotional vulnerability, practice honest communication, and experience being truly known without being abandoned or judged.

This relationship provides a template for how healthy relationships can function, with appropriate boundaries, mutual respect, and emotional safety. The therapist models healthy attachment patterns, helping the addict internalize new ways of relating that can then be applied to other relationships.

Understanding the Scope of Treatment Needed

It's crucial for therapists, partners, and addicts themselves to understand that effective treatment extends far beyond a focus on behavior modification or "addiction remediation": getting the addict to stop acting-out behaviors. While achieving sexual sobriety is an important initial goal, focusing solely on stopping unwanted behaviors is crucially inadequate for long-term recovery. Like attempting to eliminate crab grass by cutting it at the surface level, addressing only the symptomatic behaviors without treating the underlying root system ensures the problem will return.

Sexual addiction typically develops as a maladaptive coping mechanism in response to childhood trauma, neglect, or attachment disruption. The compulsive sexual behaviors are essentially symptoms of deeper wounds that remain unhealed. Comprehensive treatment must address these underlying issues—the "roots" of the addiction—or recovery will remain superficial and unstable.

What Full Recovery Looks Like

With qualified professional help, sex addicts can achieve meaningful recovery and rebuild stable, productive lives. This involves developing capacities, such as authentic intimacy, emotional regulation, and genuine empathy that may have been impaired or never fully developed because of a problematic early environment.

This comprehensive recovery process touches multiple aspects of life: rebuilding damaged relationships, developing a healthier sense of self, and learning to integrate sexuality in life-affirming rather than life-destructive ways. While the journey is challenging and requires sustained commitment, many individuals do achieve a fundamental transformation toward wholeness and authentic connection that their addiction had made impossible.

Effective Treatment: Core Components

Effective treatment for sexual addiction requires a comprehensive, multi-modal approach that addresses the complex nature of this condition. Successful recovery typically requires a combination of professional treatment and robust peer support working together to create a strong and stable recovery foundation.

A Note for Therapists and Treatment Providers

The comprehensive nature of sexual addiction treatment outlined below may initially seem daunting to clinicians considering working with this population. However, it's important to recognize that effective treatment doesn't require mastering every modality or providing every service yourself. Rather, successful treatment often involves building a network of qualified professionals and resources that can address the various aspects of recovery.

Many therapists find great satisfaction in working with sexual addiction because clients are typically highly motivated for change, having reached a point where their current life has become unmanageable. The key is starting with solid training in sexual addiction and trauma treatment, understanding your scope of practice, and knowing when and how to refer to specialists for specific aspects of care. You don't need to feel overwhelmed by the comprehensive nature of recovery; you need to feel prepared to be part of a treatment team that can support lasting healing.

Individual Therapy

Individual therapy serves as the cornerstone of sexual addiction treatment and should be conducted by a clinician specifically trained in sexual addiction and trauma treatment. This one-on-one work provides the safety and personalized attention necessary to address each person's unique history, triggers, trauma background, and recovery needs.

- **Core Areas of Focus for the Addict**

  - **Processing Childhood Trauma and Attachment Wounds**

    As noted, most sex addicts carry significant childhood trauma that created the neurobiological vulnerability underlying their addiction. Individual therapy provides a safe space to process these early experiences, whether overt abuse, emotional neglect, family addictions and dysfunction, or attachment disruptions. This work often involves grieving the childhood they never had while learning to meet their needs in healthier ways. The therapist helps the addict understand how early experiences shaped their beliefs about themselves, relationships, and sexuality.

- **Specialized Trauma Processing Modalities**

   Given the central role of trauma in sexual addiction, many therapists incorporate specialized, emotionally expressive modalities that go beyond traditional talk therapy to access and process traumatic material stored in the body and unconscious mind.

   EMDR (Eye Movement Desensitization and Reprocessing) helps process traumatic memories by using cross-brain stimulation to allow it to reprocess unresolved trauma and reduce its emotional charge. This approach is particularly effective for specific traumatic incidents or memories that continue to trigger addictive responses.

   Somatic Experiencing and Body-Based Therapies recognize that trauma is stored in the body and work to help clients develop awareness of physical sensations, release trapped trauma energy, and restore the body's natural capacity for self-regulation. Since sexual addiction often involves a disconnection from healthy bodily awareness, these approaches can be particularly healing.

Psychodrama allows clients to revisit traumatic scenes in a safe, therapeutic environment where they can experience and express the feelings they were unable to have at the time of the original trauma. With the support and witnessing of others, clients can reclaim their voice, express suppressed emotions, and gain new perspective on old wounds. This approach is particularly powerful for processing family-of-origin trauma.

Internal Family Systems (IFS) helps clients identify and heal different "parts" of themselves, including wounded inner children and protective mechanisms that may be driving addictive behaviors. This approach is especially valuable for understanding the internal conflicts that fuel sexual acting out.

Brainspotting uses specific eye positions to access and process trauma held in the subcortical brain, allowing for deep emotional release and healing without requiring extensive verbal processing.

Expressive Arts Therapy utilizes creative modalities like art, music, movement, or writing to access and express traumatic material that may be difficult to reach through words alone.

These specialized approaches recognize that trauma healing often requires accessing emotional and somatic experiences that traditional cognitive therapies may not reach, making them valuable tools in comprehensive sexual addiction treatment.

- **Developing Emotional Regulation Skills**

    Sexual acting-out often serves as a maladaptive way to manage overwhelming emotions. In therapy, addicts can learn to identify, tolerate, and regulate difficult feelings without turning to sexual behavior for relief. This includes developing mindfulness skills, learning grounding techniques to relieve anxiety, and building a vocabulary for emotional experience that may have been absent since childhood. The therapist helps the addict recognize the difference between primary emotions (the original feeling) and secondary emotions (shame about having the feeling), which is crucial for healthy emotional processing.

- **Practicing Radical Honesty**

    Individual therapy provides the safest environment for practicing the radical honesty that recovery requires. Addicts learn to tell the truth about their thoughts, feelings, and behaviors without minimizing, rationalizing, or defending. This includes learning to sit with the discomfort of being fully known, managing the shame that honesty can initially trigger, and experiencing the relief that comes from no longer maintaining exhausting secrets. The therapist's steady acceptance despite the addict's worst revelations is especially healing.

- **Identifying Personal Triggers and Risk Factors**

    Each addict has unique triggers that increase their vulnerability to acting-out: certain emotional states, relational dynamics, environmental factors, or negative thought patterns. Individual therapy helps identify these personal risk factors and develop specific strategies for managing high-risk situations. This includes creating detailed relapse prevention plans including recourse to a support network, identifying early warning signs, and developing healthy coping strategies for each identified trigger.

- **Addressing Co-occurring Mental Health Conditions**

    Many sex addicts struggle with depression, anxiety, ADHD, or other mental health conditions that may have contributed to their vulnerability to addiction. Individual therapy addresses these co-occurring conditions, often in coordination with psychiatric medication management when appropriate. Understanding how these conditions interact with sexual addiction helps create more comprehensive treatment approaches. Diagnosis of these conditions is best delayed until stable sobriety is established, as such concerns as depression and anxiety are often concomitant to active addiction and its negative consequences.

- **Creating Personalized Recovery Plans**

    Every addict needs a customized recovery plan that includes clear sobriety definitions, accountability measures, and specific strategies for maintaining sexual health. Individual therapy as well as Program sponsors help develop these personalized plans, which may include specific boundaries around technology use, social situations, travel, or other high-risk scenarios. The therapist helps the addict develop realistic expectations and sustainable practices for long-term recovery.

- **Rebuilding Healthy Sexuality**

    One of the most complex aspects of sexual addiction recovery is learning to integrate healthy sexuality while maintaining sobriety from compulsive behaviors. Individual therapy provides a safe space to explore what healthy sexuality looks like for each person, addressing distorted sexual beliefs, shame about sexuality, and the challenge of learning to tolerate and eventually develop genuine intimacy. A central component of this work involves developing the ability to stay present with themselves and their partners during intimate moments, a stark contrast to the objectification and fantasy that characterized their addictive sexual behavior. These dissociative defenses, designed to avoid the anxiety that genuine intimate connection could trigger, need to be addressed. This work often involves examining early sexual experiences, cultural or religious messages about sexuality, and developing a healthy sexual value system that emphasizes presence, mutuality, and authentic connection.

- **Developing Self-Compassion**

    Most sex addicts carry profound shame and self-hatred that actually fuels the addictive cycle. Individual therapy helps develop self-compassion: the ability to treat oneself with the same kindness one would offer a good friend. This involves learning to recognize the difference between guilt (about what one has done) and shame (about who one is), challenging internalized critical voices, and developing a more realistic and compassionate self-view.

Group Therapy

Professional group therapy led by a trained clinician provides peer support while maintaining therapeutic structure and safety. Groups typically consist of 6-8 individuals at similar stages of recovery who meet weekly for 90 minutes to 2 hours. The group setting offers particular therapeutic benefits that individual therapy alone cannot provide, creating a powerful laboratory for healing interpersonal wounds and developing authentic relational skills.

- **The Unique Power of Therapeutic Groups**

    In group therapy, participants practice new communication skills in real time, receive immediate feedback about their interpersonal patterns, and learn from others' experiences and recovery strategies. The group becomes a microcosm of the outside world where addicts can practice honesty, vulnerability, and authentic relating in a safe environment. Many sex addicts struggle with profound shame and isolation, and the group experience directly challenges these patterns by providing acceptance and understanding from peers who share similar struggles.

- **Breaking Through Isolation and Shame**

    Sexual addiction thrives in secrecy and isolation. The group environment directly counters this by creating a space where addicts can share their experiences without judgment and discover they are not uniquely damaged or alone. Hearing others articulate similar struggles, thoughts, and feelings helps normalize their experience and reduces the toxic shame that fuels addictive cycles. Many group members report that simply hearing someone else describe thoughts or behaviors they believed made them a "monster" provides profound relief and hope.

- **Learning Through Witnessing**

    Groups offer the powerful opportunity to witness others' recovery journeys at different stages. Newer members gain hope by seeing others who model longer and successful sobriety, while more experienced members reinforce their own recovery by sharing their experience and supporting newcomers. This mutual aid creates a healing community where everyone both gives and receives support.

- **Practicing Healthy Relationship Skills**

    For many sex addicts, the group may be their first experience of healthy relationships characterized by honesty, appropriate boundaries, and genuine care without a sexual agenda. Members learn to navigate conflict constructively, express needs directly, offer and receive support, and maintain relationships during difficult times. These skills can translate directly to their relationships outside the group.

- **Core Areas of Group Focus**

    Groups often focus on several key therapeutic areas that leverage the unique power of peer interaction:

    - **Processing Current Challenges and Triggers**

        Members share current struggles and receive both support and practical strategies from others who understand their experience. The group helps identify triggers, warning signs, and risk factors while developing personalized coping strategies. Having multiple perspectives on similar challenges often provides insights that individual therapy might not generate.

    - **Exploring Family-of-Origin Patterns**

        Groups provide a safe space to examine how childhood experiences and family dynamics contribute to addictive behaviors. Members often recognize patterns in others' stories that illuminate their own experiences. The group can also function as a "corrective family experience," providing the acceptance, validation, and appropriate boundaries that may have been missing in their families of origin.

- **Practicing Emotional Expression and Regulation**

    Many sex addicts have limited emotional vocabulary and difficulty tolerating intense feelings. Groups provide opportunities to practice expressing emotions safely, learning to tolerate others' emotional expression, and developing healthy ways to manage difficult feelings. Members learn that emotions can be shared and witnessed without catastrophic consequences.

- **Accountability and Sobriety Support**

    Groups provide ongoing accountability for maintaining sobriety and working recovery programs. Members check in about their sexual sobriety, share struggles with urges or slips, and receive support for getting back on track. This accountability is often more meaningful coming from peers who understand the struggle firsthand rather than solely from professionals.

- **Challenging Cognitive Distortions**

    Sex addicts often engage in thinking patterns that justify or minimize their behavior. Group members become skilled at recognizing these patterns in each other and offering gentle but direct challenges to distorted thinking (using "carefrontation" rather than confrontation). Hearing these challenges from peers who have used similar justifications can be particularly powerful.

- **The Healing Power of Witnessing**

   The witnessing aspect of group therapy, having others see and accept the addict's full story without judgment or abandonment, can be profoundly healing for individuals who have lived in secrecy and shame. Many group members describe the experience of sharing their "worst" behaviors or thoughts and receiving acceptance rather than rejection as transformative. This experience helps rewire deep beliefs about being fundamentally unlovable or irredeemably damaged.

- **Creating New Neural Pathways Through Connection**

   The group environment helps create new neural pathways associated with healthy attachment and connection. Instead of experiencing relationships as threatening or requiring deception for self-protection, group members gradually learn to associate vulnerability with safety and authentic connection with acceptance. This neurobiological shift supports long-term recovery by making healthy relationships feel possible and desirable.

- **Developing Empathy and Perspective**

   Listening to others' stories and struggles helps group members develop empathy and gain perspective on their own experiences. Many sex addicts are highly self-focused due to shame and survival mechanisms, and group participation helps expand their capacity to genuinely care for others and see beyond their own immediate concerns.

Psychoeducational Groups

Psychoeducation about sexual addiction, trauma, and recovery forms a crucial foundation for understanding the recovery process and reducing shame and self-blame. Such groups or workshops provide structured learning environments where participants gain essential knowledge while connecting with others facing similar challenges.

Psycho-ed groups typically cover the neurobiology of addiction and how addictive behaviors affect brain functioning; the relationship between childhood trauma and addictive behaviors; understanding triggers, warning signs, and the addiction cycle; healthy sexuality and the difference between addictive and authentic sexual expression; communication skills and boundary-setting; and the recovery process and what to expect in different stages of healing.

Understanding the neurobiological aspects of addiction and trauma provides hope that recovery is possible while helping both addicts and partners develop realistic expectations about the healing process. This education component often provides the first sense of hope that many people experience after the devastation of discovery.

- **Core Educational Components**

    Psychoeducational groups typically cover several fundamental areas that help participants understand their condition and the recovery process:

- **The Neurobiology of Addiction and Brain Functioning**

    Understanding how addictive behaviors literally change brain structure and function helps participants recognize that addiction is a medical condition, not a moral failing. This education covers how the reward system becomes hijacked, why willpower alone is insufficient for recovery, and how the brain can heal through sustained recovery efforts.

- **The Relationship Between Childhood Trauma and Addictive Behaviors**

    Many participants discover for the first time how early experiences shaped their neurobiological vulnerability to addiction. This education helps connect the dots between past trauma and current behaviors, reducing self-blame while highlighting the importance of trauma healing in recovery.

- **Understanding Triggers, Warning Signs, and the Addiction Cycle**

    Participants learn to identify their personal triggers and recognize the predictable patterns that lead to acting-out. Understanding the addiction cycle, from trigger to fantasy and preoccupation to acting-out to shame and back to vulnerability, helps participants interrupt these patterns more effectively. Reframing "triggers" as pointing to unhealed emotional wounds helps addicts shift the focus from blaming external stimuli for their reactivity to delving deeper into unfinished healing work that needs to be done.

- **Healthy Sexuality vs. Addictive Sexual Expression**

    Many participants have never learned what healthy sexuality looks like or how it differs from compulsive sexual behavior. This educational component covers topics like the objectification inherent in sexual acting-out, consent, mutuality, presence, and emotional connection as hallmarks of healthy sexual expression.

- **Communication Skills and Boundary-Setting**

    Practical skills training helps participants learn to express needs, set appropriate boundaries, and navigate difficult conversations. These skills that are often underdeveloped due to inadequate childhood models, trauma histories, and the focus on secrecy and deception required by addiction.

- **The Recovery Process and Stages of Healing**

    Understanding what to expect in recovery helps participants develop realistic expectations and reduces anxiety about the healing journey. This includes information about common challenges, typical timelines, and the non-linear nature of recovery progress.

- **The Power of Shared Learning**

  - **Normalizing the Experience**

    Psychoeducational groups provide relief through normalization. Participants discover that their thoughts, feelings, and behaviors are common among those with sexual addiction. Hearing that others have similar experiences reduces the sense of being uniquely damaged or "sick."

  - **Creating a Common Language**

    These groups help participants develop vocabulary for discussing their experiences, which is essential for effective therapy and communication with loved ones. Many participants have never had words for their internal experiences, and psychoeducation provides this crucial foundation.

  - **Dispelling Myths and Misconceptions**

    Many participants arrive with significant misconceptions about sexuality, addiction, and recovery, often influenced by cultural shame, religious guilt, or media portrayals. Psychoeducational groups provide accurate, science-based information that counters these harmful myths.

  - **Hope Through Understanding**

    Understanding the neurobiological aspects of addiction and trauma provides hope that recovery is possible while helping both addicts and partners develop realistic expectations about the healing process. This education component often provides the first sense of hope that many people experience after the devastation of discovery or recognition of their addiction.

- **Shifting from Shame to Science**

    When participants understand that their struggles have neurobiological underpinnings rooted in trauma and brain changes, they can begin to shift from shame-based self-condemnation to compassionate understanding of their condition. This shift is often the first step toward genuine healing.

- **Empowering Informed Decision-Making**

    Education empowers participants to make informed decisions about their treatment and recovery. Understanding various treatment options, recovery approaches, and potential challenges helps them become active participants in their healing rather than passive recipients of care.

- **Supporting Partners and Families**

    Psychoeducational groups often include partners and family members, helping them understand that sexual addiction is a genuine condition requiring professional treatment. This education can reduce blame, improve support for recovery efforts, and help loved ones develop appropriate boundaries and expectations.

- **Building Further Motivation for Treatment**

    As participants understand the complexity of their condition and the comprehensive nature of effective treatment, they often become more motivated to engage fully in the recovery process. Education helps them recognize that recovery requires both sexual sobriety and the deeper, fundamental work of trauma healing to create a pathway to transformative growth.

    The educational foundation provided by these groups creates a framework for understanding that supports all other aspects of treatment, making participants more effectively engage in therapy and more committed partners in their own recovery journey.

The Crucial Role of 12-Step Programs

12-Step programs play an indispensable role in sexual addiction recovery, providing peer support, extensive availability, spiritual growth, and a structured approach to ongoing recovery that extends far beyond formal treatment. These programs offer something that professional treatment alone cannot provide: a community of people who truly understand the experience of sexual addiction and a framework for lifelong recovery maintenance.

- **12-Step Programs for Sex Addicts:**

    Several 12-Step fellowships address sexual addiction, each with slightly different approaches and definitions of sobriety:

    Sexual Recovery Anonymous (SRA): Defines sobriety as no sex outside of a committed relationship and no masturbation.

Sex Addicts Anonymous (SAA): Uses a flexible approach where members define their own sobriety based on their specific problematic behaviors

Sexaholics Anonymous (SA): Defines sobriety as no sexual behavior outside of marriage and no masturbation or pornography use

Sex and Love Addicts Anonymous (SLAA): Addresses both sexual addiction and love addiction patterns

Sexual Compulsives Anonymous (SCA): Originally focused on gay men but now welcomes all sexual orientations. Sobriety definitions are established by the individual.

These programs provide daily structure through regular meetings, typically offering multiple meetings per week in many communities, either online or in-person. The 12 Steps provide a spiritual framework for recovery that addresses not just behavioral change but fundamental character transformation. Members work through the 12 Steps with sponsors, examining their past behaviors, making amends for harm caused, and developing a spiritual practice that supports ongoing recovery.

The fellowship aspect of 12-Step programs is particularly crucial for sex addicts, who often struggle with shame, isolation, and difficulty forming authentic relationships. Regular meeting attendance helps break through secrecy and isolation while providing models of successful recovery. Hearing others share their experiences helps normalize the addiction experience and provides hope that recovery is possible.

The program structure can offer accountability through frequent check-ins with sponsors, regular meeting attendance, and Step work that requires honest self-examination. The spiritual component addresses the spiritual bankruptcy that often accompanies active addiction, helping members develop a relationship with a higher power of their choosing that provides strength and guidance for recovery.

- **The Critical Role of Sponsorship**

    Sponsorship represents one of the most powerful elements of 12-Step recovery. A sponsor is someone with sustained recovery who guides newcomers through the 12 Steps and provides ongoing support, accountability, and mentorship. The sponsor-sponsee relationship typically involves regular contact (often daily phone calls in early recovery), working through the 12 Steps in a structured manner, and ongoing support for maintaining recovery principles. Many sponsors also encourage their sponsees to eventually sponsor others, creating a chain of recovery support that strengthens the entire fellowship and helps ensure long-term recovery by giving members a sense of purpose and service.

    These as some of the crucial benefits of working with a sponsor:

    - **Accountability:** Sponsors provide frequent check-ins and accountability for sobriety commitments, helping addicts stay honest about their struggles and progress

    - **Experience, Strength, and Hope:** Sponsors share their own recovery experience and provide guidance based on what has worked for them, offering practical wisdom about navigating recovery challenges

- **Stepwork Guidance:** Sponsors guide sponsees through the detailed work of each of the 12 Steps, providing structure and support for this challenging process of self-examination and spiritual growth

- **Crisis Support:** Sponsors are available during difficult times and can provide immediate support when the sponsee is struggling with urges, emotional difficulties, or life stresses

- **Modeling:** Sponsors demonstrate what sustained recovery looks like in practical, daily terms, showing that long-term recovery is possible

A Final Word on Treatment

The comprehensive nature of sexual addiction treatment reflects both the complexity of the condition and the profound transformation that recovery makes possible. While the journey requires commitment across multiple dimensions, including individual therapy, group work, trauma healing, group therapy, psycho-ed groups, and trauma healing, thousands of individuals have successfully navigated this path to find lives of greater authenticity, connection, and freedom than they ever thought possible.

The investment in comprehensive treatment is ultimately an investment in helping clients reclaim lives worth living, with the capacity for genuine intimacy, emotional regulation, and integrated sexuality that addiction had made impossible. Recovery is not just about helping clients stop harmful behaviors, it's about supporting them in becoming the people they were meant to be before trauma and addiction derailed their development. With proper support and sustained commitment, this transformation is not only possible but probable for the clients you serve.

9. With Alcoholism, You Just Give Up the Drug. What Do You Do with Sex Addiction . . . Give Up Sex?

This question strikes at one of the most complex aspects of sexual addiction recovery. Unlike substance addictions where complete abstinence from the addictive substance is the goal, sexual addiction recovery must navigate the challenge of developing a healthy relationship with sexuality itself. The goal is not to eliminate sexuality but to transform it from a compulsive, disconnected behavior into an expression of authentic intimacy and connection.

The Goal: Healthy, Integrated Sexuality

Healthy sexuality within the context of a mutually committed relationship is a major goal of sexual addiction recovery. This represents a fundamental shift from sexuality as an escape mechanism, emotional regulator, or way to avoid intimacy to sexuality as an expression of genuine connection, vulnerability, and mutual pleasure.

For many sex addicts, this transformation requires essentially learning healthy sexuality from the ground up. The sexual behaviors that characterized their addiction, often involving objectification, fantasy, emotional disconnection, or compulsivity, bear little resemblance to the intimate, present, and mutually satisfying sexuality that recovery aims to cultivate.

The Challenge of Childhood Trauma

Because, as noted, most sex addicts have experienced severe neglect or sexual or physical abuse in childhood, sexuality itself can be deeply problematic for the recovering individual. Childhood sexual trauma creates complex associations between sexuality and pain, powerlessness, shame, or survival that can make healthy sexual expression feel foreign or even threatening.

- **Healing Trauma as a Foundation**

    Healing childhood trauma is a necessary precursor to being able to approach sexuality with confidence and trust in recovery. This healing work must address not only overt sexual abuse but also more subtle forms of trauma such as emotional neglect, boundary violations, or exposure to inappropriate sexual material or behaviors. Until these traumatic experiences are processed and integrated, attempts at healthy sexuality may trigger trauma responses or drive individuals back toward addictive sexual behaviors as a way to manage overwhelming emotions.

- **Reclaiming the Body**

    Many trauma survivors have learned to disconnect from their bodies as a survival mechanism. Sexual addiction recovery often involves helping individuals reconnect with their physical selves in healthy ways, learning to recognize and trust bodily sensations, and developing the capacity to be present in their own skin during intimate moments.

- **The Paradox of Sexual Naivety**

    Many sex addicts are sexually naïve or unaware despite having had multiple partners or extensive sexual experiences during their acting-out years. This apparent contradiction makes sense when we understand that addictive sexual behavior is fundamentally different from healthy sexual expression.

- **Quantity vs. Quality of Experience**

    Having numerous sexual encounters doesn't translate to understanding healthy sexuality any more than having many drinks teaches someone about wine appreciation. Addictive sexual behavior is typically focused on achieving a neurochemical response, whether seeking the high of dopamine release or the numbing effect of emotional escape, rather than genuine connection, intimacy, or mutual pleasure Many sex addicts report feeling like they've been sexually active for years without ever having experienced true intimacy.

- **Learning Healthy Sexual Expression**

    Basic sexual education becomes crucial in recovery, but this education goes far beyond anatomy or technique. It involves learning about consent, communication, emotional intimacy, vulnerability, and the integration of sexuality with emotional connection. Many recovering addicts must learn how to be present during sexual activity, how to communicate their needs and boundaries, and how to experience genuine desire rather than compulsion.

    This re-education process often feels entirely foreign to individuals whose sexual experiences have been dominated by fantasy, performance anxiety, or emotional disconnection. Many must learn fundamental concepts like the difference between arousal and genuine desire, or how to recognize and communicate their authentic sexual preferences versus behaviors they engaged in compulsively. Learning to stay emotionally present during intimate moments rather than dissociating or relying on fantasy can feel uncomfortable initially but is essential for developing genuine intimacy.

    The educational component also includes understanding how healthy sexual relationships develop gradually through trust-building, emotional connection, and mutual exploration rather than the immediate intensity that characterizes addictive sexual behavior. Many recovering addicts need to learn that healthy sexuality includes saying no, setting boundaries, and prioritizing emotional safety over sexual performance. They must discover that genuine sexual satisfaction comes from connection and presence rather than conquest, novelty, or the neurochemical rush they had been seeking.

Perhaps most importantly, this sexual re-education involves learning to tolerate the vulnerability that authentic intimacy requires. For individuals who used sex to avoid emotional exposure, learning to be genuinely seen and known by a partner while being sexually intimate represents a fundamental shift from performance to authenticity, from escape to connection.

- **Developing Vulnerability Tolerance**

The development of an ability to tolerate vulnerability is essential for the integration of healthy sexuality into recovery. Addictive sexual behavior often serves as a way to avoid the vulnerability that genuine intimacy requires. Recovery involves gradually building the capacity to be emotionally present and open during sexual experiences, tolerating the uncertainty and emotional exposure that authentic intimacy demands.

For many sex addicts, the prospect of being truly seen and known during intimate moments initially feels terrifying. Their addictive behaviors have typically involved either anonymous encounters where no real self-disclosure was required, or fantasy-based sexuality that avoided the unpredictability of real human connection. Learning to maintain eye contact, engage in authentic communication during intimate moments, and allow a partner to witness their genuine emotional responses can feel overwhelmingly exposing.

This "vulnerability training" often begins outside the bedroom, as recovering addicts learn to share their authentic thoughts and feelings in nonsexual contexts. They need to practice tolerating the anxiety that comes with emotional honesty, whether expressing their recovery struggles, their fears about intimacy, or their genuine needs and desires. Many discover they have spent years using sexual behavior to avoid not just sexual vulnerability, but emotional vulnerability of any kind.

The process requires learning to distinguish between healthy vulnerability and the powerlessness they may have experienced in early traumatic situations. Many sex addicts have histories of childhood abuse or trauma that taught them that emotional exposure leads to pain or exploitation. Recovery involves learning that chosen vulnerability with a safe, caring partner is fundamentally different from the helpless exposure they may have experienced in the past.

Gradually, as recovering addicts develop the ability to be emotionally present without escaping into fantasy or performance, they often discover that the vulnerability they once feared actually deepens their capacity for pleasure, connection, and satisfaction. The authentic intimacy that emerges from mutual vulnerability creates a form of sexual and emotional fulfillment that their addictive behaviors never provided, making the difficult work of developing vulnerability tolerance ultimately transformative.

- **The Role of Couples Therapy**

Couple's therapy is often essential for partners to develop sufficient healing and reestablishment of trust for intimate relations to resume. The betrayal trauma experienced by partners creates legitimate barriers to sexual intimacy that must be addressed before healthy sexual connection can be restored.

- **Rebuilding Trust and Safety**

    Partners need time and support to heal from betrayal trauma before they can feel safe being sexually intimate again. This process cannot be rushed, and attempting to restore sexual intimacy before adequate trust has been rebuilt often re-traumatizes partners and undermines recovery efforts.

    The timeline for this healing varies dramatically among partners, potentially taking months or even years depending on the extent of the betrayal, the partner's trauma history, and the quality of the recovery process. During this period, partners may experience physical reactions to sexual contact including panic attacks, flashbacks, or emotional numbing that make sexual intimacy feel impossible or even harmful. Their bodies may have learned to associate sexual touch with danger, deception, and emotional pain.

Many partners describe feeling like their sexuality has been "contaminated" by their partner's addiction. They may struggle with intrusive thoughts during intimate moments, wondering where their partner's hands have been, whether they're being compared to others, or if their partner is fantasizing about someone else. These trauma responses are normal and protective, signs that their nervous system is trying to prevent further harm by remaining hypervigilant during moments of physical vulnerability.

The healing process often requires partners to reclaim their own sexuality separate from their relationship. This might involve individual therapy to process trauma responses, learning to reconnect with their own body through non-sexual touch, or exploring what they actually want and need sexually versus what they previously accommodated to keep peace in the relationship. Many partners discover they had suppressed their own authentic sexual desires to avoid triggering their partner's acting out or to maintain the illusion of sexual compatibility.

Premature attempts at sexual reconnection often backfire because they force partners to override their natural protective responses before genuine safety has been established. When partners push themselves to be sexual before they're ready, whether due to pressure from their partner, misguided therapist, or their own desire to "fix" the relationship, they often experience re-traumatization that can set the healing process back significantly. This can create additional shame and feelings of failure that complicate both individual and relationship recovery.

True sexual healing requires that partners feel genuine choice and control over their sexual experiences, something that may have been absent during the active addiction. They need to know they can say no without consequence, set boundaries without argument, and express their trauma responses without being criticized or rushed. Only when this foundation of safety and choice is solidly established can authentic sexual intimacy begin to be carefully and gradually rebuilt.

- **Creating New Sexual Scripts**

    Couples often need to develop entirely new approaches to sexual intimacy that are distinct from patterns established during the addiction. This may involve learning new ways to initiate intimacy, communicate during sexual activity, and integrate emotional connection with physical expression.

    This process of creating new sexual scripts requires dismantling patterns that may have been established over years or even decades. During the active addiction, sexual interactions may have been characterized by emotional distance, performance pressure, secrecy, or the addict's covert attempts to recreate pornographic scenarios. Partners may have learned to suppress their own desires, accommodate behaviors that felt uncomfortable, or disconnect emotionally to protect themselves from further hurt.

The new scripts must prioritize mutual consent, emotional safety, and authentic desire over performance or fantasy recreation. This often means slowing down the sexual process significantly, creating space for check-ins and communication that may feel awkward initially but become essential for rebuilding trust. Couples may need to learn how to talk during intimate moments, expressing what feels good, what doesn't, what they need, or when they need to pause.

Many couples discover they need to completely reimagine how sexual encounters begin. Instead of the goal-oriented, performance-focused approach that may have characterized their previous sexual relationship, they learn to prioritize emotional connection and presence. This might involve extended periods of non-sexual intimacy like cuddling, massage, or simply talking before any sexual activity occurs.

The integration of emotional connection with physical expression often requires explicit practice and patience. Many couples find they need to learn how to maintain eye contact during intimate moments, share their feelings verbally during sexual activity, and stay present with each other rather than escaping into individual fantasy. This emotional integration can initially feel vulnerable and uncomfortable for both partners, but ultimately creates the foundation for authentic intimacy.

Creating these new scripts also involves establishing clear agreements about boundaries, preferences, and limitations that honor both partners' healing process. This might include agreements about specific activities, timing, initiation methods, or communication practices that support both the addict's recovery and the partner's trauma healing. These scripts are not rigid rules but evolving agreements that can be adjusted as both partners heal and grow in their capacity for healthy intimacy.

- **The Value of Initial Abstinence**

Often, an initial period of abstinence is recommended to give both parties time to sort out their feelings about sexuality and to develop an understanding of what constitutes healthy, sober sexual expression. This therapeutic abstinence serves several important functions in early recovery.

   - **Breaking Compulsive Patterns**

   A period of sexual abstinence helps break the neurological patterns associated with compulsive sexual behavior, allowing the brain to begin forming new, healthier associations with intimacy and connection.

   - **Focusing on Emotional Intimacy**

   Removing sexual activity temporarily allows couples to focus on rebuilding emotional intimacy, communication, and trust without the complexity that sexual interaction can add during early recovery. Many couples discover forms of intimacy and connection they had never experienced when sexual behavior was driven by addiction rather than genuine desire.

- **Developing Sexual Sobriety**

Just as someone recovering from alcoholism must learn what sober living looks like, sex addicts must develop an understanding of what sexual sobriety means for them. This period of abstinence provides space to develop personal definitions of healthy sexuality and to distinguish between genuine desire and addictive urges. Additionally, sexual abstinence often serves as a revealing process, bringing to the surface underlying emotions such as anxiety, depression, loneliness, or trauma that the sexual behavior may have been masking or helping to avoid.

Without the familiar escape of compulsive sexual activity, individuals are confronted with these previously numbed feelings, which can feel overwhelming and intense. These newly surfaced emotions require careful management and therapeutic support, as their sudden emergence can trigger relapse if not properly addressed. Learning healthy coping strategies, building emotional tolerance, and developing new ways to process difficult feelings becomes crucial for maintaining sobriety during this vulnerable period, ultimately creating an opportunity for genuine emotional processing and healing that is essential for long-term recovery.

- **Partner Healing**

    For betrayed partners, a period of sexual abstinence provides necessary time to heal from trauma responses and rebuild the sense of safety required for consensual intimate connection. As noted, rushing back into sexual intimacy often retraumatizes partners and undermines their healing process.

- **The Possibility of Transformed Intimacy**

Over time, couples who have committed to the necessary recovery work often report that their sexual connection has reached a new-found depth of intimacy that far exceeds anything they experienced before. Many describe discovering dimensions of emotional and physical connection they never knew were possible: a sense of being truly seen, known, and accepted by their partner in ways that transcend mere physical gratification.

This deeper intimacy often encompasses not just sexual encounters but extends to everyday interactions, communication, and emotional vulnerability. Partners frequently report feeling more present with each other, experiencing heightened trust, and finding that their physical intimacy is now grounded in genuine emotional safety rather than compulsion or performance.

The contrast between addictive sexual behavior and this

transformed intimacy can be striking: where addiction created distance and secrecy, recovery fosters transparency and closeness; where compulsion drove disconnected encounters, healing enables truly intimate union. This transformation represents one of the most profound gifts of comprehensive sexual addiction recovery, offering couples the possibility of a relationship that is more fulfilling and authentic than what either partner may have previously thought achievable.

- **From Compulsion to Choice**

    Healthy sexuality in recovery is characterized by choice rather than compulsion, presence rather than escape, and connection rather than objectification. Many recovering couples describe experiencing sexuality as an expression of their emotional bond rather than a separate or disconnected activity.

    - **Integrated Intimacy**

        Recovery creates the possibility for integrated intimacy where emotional, physical, and spiritual connection merge into a holistic experience of closeness. This integration often feels completely foreign to couples whose sexual relationship was previously characterized by addiction, but it represents the goal toward which recovery efforts are directed.

- **Deeper Satisfaction Through Hard-Won Trust**

    For couples who successfully navigate the challenging process of rebuilding trust and emotional safety, many report that the level of satisfaction with their intimate connection increases dramatically in recovery. This transformation doesn't happen automatically or quickly. It requires extensive relational healing, consistent accountability from the addict, and careful attention to the partner's trauma recovery needs.

    Partners who felt rejected and unwanted during the addiction, when the active addict was often disinterested in genuine intimacy may eventually experience a level of desire and attention that had been absent for years. However, this renewed intimacy is only possible after substantial trust has been rebuilt through sustained recovery efforts, transparent communication, and the addict's demonstrated commitment to change.

- **The Promise and Reality of Sexual Recovery**

The quality of connection, presence, and mutual care that can characterize healthy sexuality often creates more satisfying intimate experiences than anything the couple had known before the addiction took hold. Yet this outcome represents the successful completion of extensive healing work, not an inevitable result of stopping addictive behaviors. Many couples require months or even years of individual and couples therapy, with no guarantee that sexual intimacy will be restored to either partner's satisfaction.

The journey from addictive sexual behavior to healthy, integrated sexuality is complex and requires patience, professional support, and commitment from both partners. However, the possibility of experiencing sexuality as a genuine expression of love, connection, and mutual pleasure makes this challenging transformation one of the most rewarding aspects of sexual addiction and betrayal trauma recovery.

10. Isn't Sexuality a Private Matter? Why Should We Care Whether or Not Someone Is a Sex Addict?

This question strikes at the heart of a crucial distinction that many people fail to understand: Sex is a private matter; sexual addiction is not. While healthy sexual expression between consenting adults deserves privacy and respect, sexual addiction inevitably extends far beyond the bedroom, creating ripple effects that impact families, workplaces, institutions, communities, and society as a whole.

- **The Public Consequences of "Private" Behavior**

    Sexual addiction rarely remains contained within the private sphere. Its compulsive nature drives behaviors that inevitably spill over into public life, affecting others who never consented to be part of the addictive cycle:

115

- **Financial Devastation**

    When the head of a household secretly drains the family's finances because he patronizes prostitutes, the entire family suffers the consequences. Children may lose their college funds, families may face foreclosure, and spouses may discover they have no savings or retirement security, all because of behaviors they knew nothing about. The financial cost of sexual addiction can include spending on pornography, escort services, "sugar baby" arrangements, webcam sex, massage parlours and sex clubs, sex toys, hotel rooms, travel for sexual encounters, and even legal fees when behaviors cross legal boundaries.

- **Professional, Familial, and Institutional Damage**

    When a respected politician is caught in a sexual sting, public trust in government erodes. When an executive sexually repeatedly harasses her subordinates, workplace safety and productivity suffer while the organization faces legal liability. When a clergyman is promiscuous among his congregation, the spiritual foundation of an entire community is shattered. When the president of a university loses his post because he is caught making obscene phone calls, the institution's reputation and effectiveness are compromised.

    When a sex scandal involving a public figure erupts into national headlines, it often becomes a source of passing entertainment or political fodder for the public, a titillating distraction from daily life that generates water cooler conversations and social media commentary. However, behind the sensationalized coverage and partisan debates lies a trail of devastating personal destruction that rarely receives adequate attention. The spouse who discovers years of deception experiences profound betrayal trauma that can take years to heal. Children watch their family disintegrate under the glare of public scrutiny, carrying shame and confusion that may affect their ability to trust and form healthy relationships for decades. Colleagues and employees lose their jobs when institutions collapse under scandal, while constituents or congregation members who believed in their leader's integrity face a crisis of faith in the very systems they trusted.

The financial costs of legal proceedings, settlements, and institutional damage can reach millions of dollars, but the human cost, measured in broken families, shattered trust, and damaged communities, extends far beyond what any headline can capture. What appears as a momentary scandal in the news cycle often represents years or even generations of healing required for those whose lives were upended by one person's sexual addiction.

- **Family Destruction**

When a parent goes cruising in the middle of the night, children are left wondering why Mom or Dad disappeared, the family lives with unexplained tension, and the fundamental safety and security that children need for healthy development is undermined. These children often develop hypervigilance, constantly scanning their environment for signs of danger or abandonment. They may blame themselves for their parent's absence, wondering what they did wrong to drive their parent away. The addicted parent's emotional unavailability, even when physically present, creates an atmosphere of chronic stress and confusion.

Children in these families frequently become parentified, taking on adult responsibilities to fill the void left by the absent or emotionally unavailable parent. They may find themselves comforting the non-addicted parent, caring for younger siblings, or trying to manage household responsibilities beyond their developmental capacity. The unpredictability of the addicted parent's behavior, often loving and attentive one day, absent or irritable the next, teaches children that relationships are inherently unstable and unsafe.

The trauma extends to multiple generations as children grow up with attachment wounds and distorted views of relationships and sexuality. These children often struggle with their own intimate relationships as adults, either becoming hypervigilant about potential betrayal or unconsciously choosing partners who replicate the emotional unavailability they experienced in childhood. Many develop their own addictive behaviors, having learned that substances or compulsive behaviors can provide temporary relief from emotional pain. The family patterns of secrecy, denial, and emotional distance become normalized, creating a legacy that can persist for generations until someone breaks the cycle through intentional healing work.

- **Cultural Impact**

    When a sports hero boasts in the media of having more than a thousand sexual conquests, young people receive messages that sexual objectification and conquest are admirable. These public displays of sexual flaunting normalize compulsive sexual behavior and contribute to a culture that increasingly struggles to distinguish between healthy sexuality and addictive exploitation. Young men learn that masculinity is measured by the number of sexual partners they accumulate, while young women internalize that their primary value lies in their sexual availability and appeal to men.

    The celebration of sexual scores in media and popular culture teaches adolescents that sex is about power, performance, and accumulation rather than intimacy, connection, and mutual respect. When famous athletes, entertainers, or other public figures are praised for their sexual exploits rather than critiqued for their objectification of others, it sends a clear message that treating people as sexual objects is not only acceptable but worthy of admiration. This cultural messaging becomes particularly dangerous in the internet age, where young people have unprecedented access to pornographic content that reinforces these distorted values.

The normalization of sexual addiction in popular culture also makes it increasingly difficult for young people to recognize problematic sexual behavior in themselves or others. When compulsive sexual behavior is portrayed as normal male sexuality or when the exploitation of others is presented as sexual liberation, young people lose the framework for understanding what healthy sexuality actually looks like. This cultural shift affects dating relationships, creates unrealistic expectations about sexual performance and frequency, and contributes to the objectification and sexualization of women and girls in everyday interactions.

Furthermore, when sexual addiction is glamorized rather than recognized as a serious mental health condition, it becomes harder for those struggling with compulsive sexual behavior to seek help. The cultural message that "more is always better" when it comes to sexual partners or sexual activity prevents people from recognizing when their behavior has become compulsive and destructive. This cultural normalization extends the struggles of those trapped in sexual addiction while increasing the likelihood that others will develop similar patterns.

- **The Expanding Scope of Impact**

The following examples represent just a few instances of the devastating impact of sexual addiction on our corporate, athletic, political, religious, and family institutions. The consequences extend far beyond the individual addict:

- **Betrayal Trauma in Families**

Partners of sex addicts experience severe betrayal trauma that can last for years, affecting their ability to trust, form relationships, and function effectively in their personal and professional lives. This trauma is particularly devastating because it comes from the person who was supposed to be their greatest source of safety and support. Partners often describe feeling like their entire reality has been shattered, as they discover that years or even decades of their life were built on lies and deception. The systematic gaslighting that typically accompanies sexual addiction leaves partners questioning their own perceptions, memories, and sanity.

The symptoms of betrayal trauma mirror those of post-traumatic stress disorder and can include intrusive thoughts about the partner's sexual activities, hypervigilance about potential deception, emotional numbing, panic attacks, and physical symptoms like insomnia and digestive problems. Many partners develop an inability to concentrate at work, leading to decreased job performance and sometimes job loss at the very time they may need financial independence most. Their social relationships suffer as they struggle with shame about their situation and difficulty trusting others. The intimate relationship skills they once possessed, such as vulnerability, emotional openness, sexual spontaneity, may feel dangerous and impossible to access.

Children in these families often develop attachment disorders, anxiety, depression, and their own relationship difficulties that can persist into adulthood. Even when parents believe they are successfully hiding the addiction from their children, kids are remarkably perceptive and pick up on the tension, arguments, and emotional distance between their parents. They may not understand what's happening, but they feel the disruption that's occurring, often blaming themselves for their family's problems and experiencing anxiety about the family's stability.

As these children mature into adolescence and young adulthood, they often struggle with their own intimate relationships. Having learned that love comes with deception and that the people closest to you can't be trusted, they may either avoid relationships entirely or unconsciously choose partners who replicate the emotional unavailability they experienced at home. Many develop their own addictive behaviors as coping mechanisms, perpetuating the cycle of dysfunction into the next generation. The trauma they experienced in childhood can affect their ability to form secure attachments, communicate effectively in relationships, and trust their own instincts about people and situations.

- **Workplace Disruption**

  Sexual addiction in the workplace creates hostile environments, reduces productivity, increases turnover, and exposes organizations to significant legal and financial liability. When employees engage in repetitive inappropriate sexual behaviors that resist correction, patterns that likely indicate underlying sexual addiction, it creates misconduct that is particularly damaging to workplace culture and safety. Unlike isolated incidents of poor judgment, the compulsive nature of sexual addiction means that problematic behaviors often escalate and repeat despite warnings, training, or disciplinary action. Most employees today have been well-trained in appropriate workplace sexual behavior, but the sex addict is someone who, although aware, cannot consistently abide by these guidelines.

The time, energy, and resources required to address sexual harassment, inappropriate behavior, and the aftermath of sexual misconduct divert attention from organizational missions and goals. Human resources departments find themselves spending countless hours investigating complaints, documenting incidents, and managing the fallout from repeated inappropriate behaviors. Legal costs can mount quickly, not only from potential lawsuits but also from the need for specialized legal counsel to navigate complex employment law issues. Organizations may face regulatory investigations, consent decrees, and ongoing monitoring that can last for years.

The financial costs compound over time, including not only direct legal expenses and potential settlements but also the hidden costs of increased turnover, reduced productivity, damaged reputation, and the expense of implementing enhanced training and monitoring systems. For organizations in regulated industries, sexual misconduct can trigger regulatory scrutiny that affects licensing, contracts, and business relationships. When the inappropriate behavior involves someone in a leadership position, the entire organization may face existential threats as stakeholders lose confidence in the institution's ability to govern itself effectively.

A recent example illustrates this dynamic: In 2024, San Diego Unified School District, California's second-largest school district, fired Superintendent Lamont Jackson after an investigation substantiated allegations of sexual misconduct with female staff. The scandal revealed what reporters called "a damning revelation" that district officials weren't just failing to prevent sexual misconduct but were engaging in it themselves. The aftermath left the institution struggling to rebuild trust among stakeholders and forcing a fundamental reckoning about the district's culture and leadership capabilities.

- **Economic Costs**

The societal cost of sexual addiction includes not only direct financial losses but also the expenses associated with legal proceedings, treatment programs, family court interventions, and the social services required to address the fallout. When families are destroyed by sexual addiction, the community often bears the cost of supporting single-parent households, providing mental health services for traumatized family members, and addressing the educational and social needs of affected children.

These economic impacts ripple through multiple systems simultaneously. The legal system becomes burdened with complex divorce proceedings that often involve disputes over assets, custody battles complicated by addiction issues, and sometimes criminal cases when sexual addiction involves illegal activities. Family courts require specialized personnel trained in addiction and trauma issues, and cases often drag on for months or years, consuming substantial judicial resources. Child protective services may become involved when children are exposed to inappropriate sexual material or situations requiring investigations, ongoing monitoring, and sometimes temporary or permanent placement in foster care.

Both families and healthcare systems absorb significant costs treating the physical and mental health consequences of sexual addiction and its impact on families. Partners may require specialized therapy for betrayal trauma, children may need counseling for attachment disorders and anxiety, and the addicted individuals themselves will require comprehensive treatment that may include multiple residential stays, ongoing therapy, and medical care for sexually transmitted infections or other health complications. Insurance systems struggle to adequately cover these specialized treatments, often leaving families with substantial out-of-pocket expenses at the very time their financial resources have been impacted by the addiction. The economic burden extends to employers who face increased healthcare costs, reduced productivity from affected employees, and the costs of employee assistance programs.

When calculated across all these systems, the true economic cost of sexual addiction to society likely exceeds billions of dollars annually, making investment in prevention and early intervention programs not just a moral imperative but an economic necessity.

- **Erosion of Trust in Institutions**

Each high-profile case of sexual misconduct among leaders and public figures, whether or not it is publicly labeled as sexual addiction, further erodes public trust in the institutions that form the foundation of civil society. The repetitive, compulsive patterns characteristic of sexual addiction often underlie these scandals, but the public typically sees only the surface behaviors: the affairs, the harassment allegations, the inappropriate relationships with subordinates, or the criminal charges. What appears as moral failing or poor judgment to the public may actually represent the manifestation of untreated sexual addiction, but this underlying condition rarely receives recognition or discussion in media coverage.

Whether in government, religion, education, sports, or business, patterns of sexual misconduct among leaders create cynicism and undermine the social fabric that holds communities together. When a respected politician is caught in multiple affairs, when a beloved teacher is arrested for inappropriate relationships with students, when a trusted financial advisor is discovered to have been exploiting clients sexually, or when a religious leader is exposed for serial sexual promiscuity among his congregation, the damage extends far beyond the immediate victims. The public watches these scandals unfold and begins to question whether any leader can be trusted, whether any institution is actually committed to the values it espouses.

The cumulative effect of repeated high-profile sexual scandals creates a culture of cynicism that affects civic engagement and social cohesion. The tragedy is that many of these scandals might be preventable if sexual addiction were better understood and treated before it manifests in public misconduct. However, because the underlying addiction is rarely identified or addressed, society continues to treat these incidents as isolated moral failures rather than symptoms of a treatable condition. This misunderstanding perpetuates a cycle where sexual addiction remains hidden until it explodes into public scandal, taking down not only the individual but damaging the institutions and communities they were supposed to serve.

The Internet Age: Amplifying the Crisis

Education about the costs of sexual addiction to all of our institutions becomes ever more important in the internet age. The digital revolution has fundamentally changed the landscape of sexual addiction, making problematic sexual content more accessible than ever before while normalizing behaviors that previous generations would have recognized as clearly addictive. What once required significant effort, expense, and risk to access is now available instantly and privately, creating conditions that can rapidly accelerate the development of sexual addiction and make recovery more challenging.

The internet has not only democratized access to sexual content but has also created new forms of sexual acting-out that didn't exist before the digital age. Online sexual behaviors like cybersex, cam-to-cam interactions, sexting, virtual affairs, and consumption of live-streamed sexual content have expanded the repertoire of potentially addictive behaviors far beyond what was possible in previous generations. These digital behaviors can feel less "real" to participants, creating a false sense of safety that allows people to escalate into more extreme or risky behaviors than they might attempt in person.

- **The Triple Threat: Accessibility, Affordability, and Anonymity**

    The internet has created what researchers call the "Triple A Engine" (Affordability, Anonymity, and Accessibility) that accelerates the development of sexual addiction in unprecedented ways. This combination of factors has created a perfect storm for the proliferation of compulsive sexual behavior across all demographics and age groups.

- **Affordability: The Economic/Effort Barriers Eliminated**

    Affordability means that vast amounts of sexual content are immediately and easily available for free or at minimal cost, removing the barriers that once limited access to sexually explicit material. Where previous generations might have needed to travel to purchase magazines, videos, or pay for adult entertainment venues, today's internet users can access unlimited pornographic content without financial investment or effort. This economic accessibility and effortless acquisition has eliminated what were once natural brake on consumption, allowing individuals to escalate their viewing habits without the reality check of mounting expenses or inconvenience. The financial "invisibility" of free content also makes it easier for individuals to rationalize their consumption and harder for partners to detect escalating behavior through financial records or the presence of physical products.

- **Anonymity: The Removal of Social Accountability**

    Anonymity allows people to engage in sexual behaviors online without the social constraints that might otherwise limit their actions. The privacy of internet use means that individuals can explore sexual content and behaviors without fear of social judgment, professional consequences, or relationship accountability—at least initially. This perceived anonymity can lead people to engage in sexual behaviors online that they would never consider in face-to-face situations.

For sex addicts, the internet becomes akin to a labyrinth, where it is possible to wander deeper and deeper in a search for new content as tolerance develops for previously stimulating materials. This digital maze creates a pathway toward increasingly extreme content, with addicts sometimes reporting that they eventually turned to off-limits material that previously was not part of their sexual repertoire. The addictive brain's constant demand for novelty finds endless fuel in the internet's vast array of sexual content, making it easy to drift from relatively benign material into content that violates personal values and legal boundaries.

However, this sense of anonymity is often illusory, as digital footprints can be traced, and the psychological and relational consequences of online sexual behavior are very real. The false sense of invisibility can lead to increasingly risky behaviors, including illegal activities, that can have devastating long-term consequences. For some families, the shattering of this illusion comes in the most traumatic way possible, when law enforcement arrives at their door with arrest warrants, seizing computers and phones as evidence in cases involving illegal material such as child pornography. Children may witness a parent being taken away in handcuffs, while spouses are left to grapple with the dual shock of their partner's arrest and the realization of behaviors they never suspected. What has felt private and consequence-free in the moment can destroy careers, marriages, and lives when the reality of digital permanence becomes apparent, leaving entire families to navigate the devastating aftermath of actions that began behind a computer screen.

- **Accessibility: The 24/7 Availability**

Accessibility means that sexual content and opportunities for sexual acting out are available 24/7 from any location with internet access. This constant availability transforms sexual acting-out from something that once required planning and specific circumstances to something that can happen impulsively at any moment. The ubiquity of smartphones means that sexual content is literally always within reach: in the workplace, at home, in cars, on vacation, or during any moment of boredom, stress, or emotional difficulty. This constant availability makes it extremely difficult for individuals struggling with sexual addiction to create the environmental controls that are often necessary for recovery.

The always-on nature of internet access also means that sexual acting out can interfere with sleep, work, family time, and other essential life activities in ways that were previously impossible. People can now engage in sexual behaviors during work hours, in the middle of the night, or during family events, creating significant disruption to their daily functioning and relationships. The portability of access through mobile devices has essentially made it impossible to create "safe" spaces free from sexual triggers and opportunities.

- **The Normalization of Extreme Content**

The internet has not only made sexual content more available but has also dramatically escalated the intensity and extremity of what is considered "normal." Content that would have been considered hardcore pornography just decades ago is now mainstream, and young people are being exposed to increasingly violent, degrading, and unrealistic portrayals of sexuality as their primary source of sexual education.

This normalization of extreme content has profound implications for how entire generations understand sexuality, consent, and relationships. Pornographic content now routinely depicts violence against women as pleasurable, presents degrading sexual acts as standard practices, and portrays women as objects whose primary purpose is male sexual gratification. What was once found only in the most extreme corners of adult entertainment has migrated into mainstream pornography, creating a cultural shift where aggression, dominance, and the objectification of women have become normalized aspects of sexual expression.

The impact on young people is particularly alarming, as many encounter this content before they have developed critical thinking skills about sexuality or formed their own values about healthy relationships. Instead of learning about mutual respect, emotional intimacy, and genuine consent, young people are absorbing messages that sex is about power, performance, and the submission of one partner to another's desires. The pornographic "education" they receive teaches boys that masculinity is demonstrated through sexual dominance and aggression, while teaching girls that their value lies in their willingness to submit to increasingly extreme sexual demands.

This distorted sexual education contributes directly to the emergence of what some researchers call misogynistic "bro culture" in schools, colleges, and young adult social circles. When pornography becomes the primary teacher about sexuality, it creates generations of young men who view women as sexual objects rather than equal partners, and who believe that aggressive or degrading sexual behavior is not only acceptable but expected. Young women, meanwhile, may internalize the message that they should tolerate or even enjoy treatment that previous generations would have recognized as abusive. The consequences extend far beyond individual relationships into broader cultural attitudes about women and sexuality. When extreme content becomes normalized, it shifts the baseline for what society considers acceptable sexual behavior.

The unrealistic expectations created by pornographic content also contribute to sexual dysfunction and relationship problems among young adults. When sexual performance is measured against pornographic standards rather than mutual satisfaction and emotional connection, both men and women may struggle with feelings of inadequacy, performance anxiety, and disconnection from their own authentic sexual desires. The result is a generation that may be more sexually active but less sexually satisfied than their predecessors.

- **The Crisis of Early Exposure**

Perhaps nowhere is the public health impact of sexual addiction more concerning than in its effect on children and adolescents. The average age of first exposure to online pornography is now 11 years old, meaning that children are encountering sexually explicit material before they have developed the cognitive, emotional, or psychological tools to process these experiences appropriately. This represents a fundamental shift in childhood development, as an entire generation is being exposed to adult sexual content during critical periods of brain development when their understanding of relationships, intimacy, and sexuality is still forming.

The timing of this exposure is particularly damaging because it occurs during pre-adolescence, when children are naturally curious about sexuality but lack the cognitive maturity to distinguish between fantasy and reality, or between healthy and unhealthy sexual expression. At age 11, most children have not yet experienced romantic relationships, may not have received comprehensive sexual education, and are still developing their sense of personal boundaries and values. When pornographic content becomes their first "teacher" about sexuality, it creates a distorted foundation that can influence their sexual development for years to come.

What makes this exposure particularly concerning is that it is often accidental rather than intentional. Children searching for innocent content online may stumble across explicit material through pop-up ads, mislabeled websites, or search results that were not filtered appropriately. This means that their first exposure to sexuality often occurs without any context, preparation, or adult guidance to help them process what they've seen. The shock and confusion that can result from unexpected exposure to explicit content can be traumatic for children, particularly when the content depicts violence, degradation, or extreme sexual acts.

The neurobiological impact of early pornography exposure cannot be overstated. During childhood and adolescence, the brain is still developing, particularly in areas responsible for impulse control, decision-making, and the formation of neural pathways related to reward and pleasure. Exposure to the intense stimulation provided by pornographic content during these critical developmental periods can literally rewire the developing brain, creating neural pathways that associate sexual arousal with the specific content and patterns they encountered during their formative years.

This neurobiological imprinting helps explain why individuals who are exposed to pornography at young ages often struggle with sexual dysfunction, sexual addiction, and relationship difficulties as adults. Their brains learned to respond to artificial, extreme stimulation during development, making it difficult to become aroused by the more subtle, intimate experiences that characterize healthy adult relationships. The result is often a generation of young adults who require increasingly extreme content to achieve sexual arousal and who struggle to form satisfying intimate relationships with real partners.

- **Educational Displacement**

  For many young people, pornography serves as their primary source of sexual education, replacing age-appropriate information about healthy sexuality, consent, and emotional intimacy with content designed to be sexually arousing rather than educational. This creates a generation of young people whose understanding of sexuality is fundamentally shaped by addictive and exploitative content designed to be arousing rather than to offer accurate, healthy information about human sexuality and relationships.

  The consequences of this miseducation are profound and

long-lasting. Instead of learning that healthy sexuality involves communication, emotional connection, and gradual exploration between caring, equal partners, young people learn that sex is a performance focused on physical acts rather than emotional intimacy. They absorb lessons about sexual techniques without context about consent, communication, or the emotional preparation necessary for healthy sexual experiences. The result is a generation that may be technically knowledgeable about sexual acts but fundamentally ignorant about healthy sexual relationships.

Perhaps most damaging is how pornography teaches young people that sexual satisfaction comes from increasingly extreme acts rather than from emotional connection and mutual care. This progression mirrors the trajectory of sexual addiction itself, where tolerance and escalation drive users toward more shocking and extreme content to achieve the same arousal. Research demonstrates that disturbing and even disgusting pornographic images actually trigger larger dopamine releases than conventional sexual content, the very neurochemical response that fuels addictive behavior. As young people's brains become conditioned to expect heightened stimulation, they may find normal, healthy sexual experiences insufficient to create arousal, setting the stage for addictive patterns that prioritize increasingly extreme content over genuine intimacy.

This creates unrealistic expectations about sexual

performance and frequency that can make real relationships feel inadequate or boring by comparison. Young people may enter their first sexual relationships expecting their partners to behave like pornographic performers, leading to disappointment, pressure, and often harmful sexual practices that prioritize performance over pleasure, safety, or emotional well-being.

This educational crisis extends beyond individual relationships to affect broader social attitudes about sexuality. When an entire generation receives its sexual education from pornographic content, it normalizes exploitation, objectification, and aggression as acceptable aspects of sexual expression. The result is a cultural shift away from viewing sexuality as an expression of love and intimacy toward viewing it as a recreational activity focused on power, dominance, and physical gratification.

- **Addiction Development**

    Perhaps most concerning about early exposure to pornography is that it significantly increases the risk of developing sexual addiction later in life. The developing adolescent brain is particularly vulnerable to addictive processes, and early exposure to the intense neurochemical stimulation provided by pornographic content can establish addictive patterns that persist into adulthood. This vulnerability stems from the fundamental differences between adolescent and adult brain development. Adolescence represents one of the most active and critical times of brain development. The adolescent brain is highly impressionable and vulnerable to forming patterns of behavior. During this time, the brain is establishing the foundations of neural pathways that contribute to long-term brain development.

The neurobiological mechanisms underlying this increased vulnerability are well-documented. When pornography exposure occurs at younger ages, it is influential in developing arousal templates and programming sexual scripts that become deeply embedded in the developing neural architecture. The adolescent brain's reward system, which is still maturing, becomes conditioned to respond to the artificial hyperstimulation of pornographic content during a critical period when neural pathways are being established for life.

Studies have reported that this early conditioning can lead to profound changes in sexual behavior and preferences. While research in this area varies in methodology and scope, available studies indicate concerning patterns where regular pornography users can develop habitual usage patterns, with some reporting decreased interest in real-life partnerships, preferring virtual experiences that they view as more convenient and tailored to specific desires. This indicates the possibility that a fundamental rewiring of sexual motivation away from human connection toward artificial stimulation is occurring.

The relationship between early exposure and later problems follows a clear pattern: the more exposure, the more problems. Research has found that "sexually explicit media exposure in early adolescence was strongly related to three risky sexual behaviors (early sexual debut, unsafe sex, and multiple sexual partners) in late adolescence, and this relationship was very close to causal." In other words, young people who consumed more types of sexual media, whether videos, images, websites, or other formats, were significantly more likely to engage in risky sexual behaviors as they got older. This pattern suggests that pornography exposure doesn't just happen to occur alongside these problems; it actually contributes to causing them.

The neuroplastic changes that occur during adolescent exposure to pornography can establish addiction patterns that become progressively more difficult to change with age. Studies have found that these changes are associated with dysphoria and depressed mood related to the addictive behavior, as well as loss of self-control and internal conflict, symptoms that researchers note bear similarity to those seen in obsessive-compulsive disorders, particularly the intrusive, repetitive nature of compulsive sexual thoughts and the difficulty stopping the behavior despite negative consequences. Critically, during this vulnerable developmental period, these neuroplastic changes shape how the brain's reward system responds to sexual stimuli. The developing brain essentially learns that sexual arousal and pleasure are tied to pornographic imagery rather than intimate human connection, creating a neurobiological foundation for sexual addiction that can persist throughout life if not addressed with appropriate treatment.

This understanding of early exposure as a primary risk factor for sexual addiction underscores the critical importance of protecting children from pornographic content during their developmental years. The neurobiological vulnerability of the adolescent brain means that exposure during this period can have lifelong consequences that extend far beyond the immediate viewing experience.

- **Why We Must Care**

The question "Why should we care whether someone is a sex addict?" answers itself when we understand the extensive ways that sexual addiction impacts society. We care because:

- **No One Consents to Be Collateral Damage**

While sexual behavior between consenting adults deserves privacy, sexual addiction inevitably involves people who never consented to be affected by someone else's compulsive sexual behavior. Spouses, children, coworkers, and community members all suffer consequences they did not choose and cannot control.

This fundamental violation of consent extends far beyond the boundaries of the addicted individual's private life. Spouses discover that their financial security has been compromised by spending on pornography, escort services, or sex tourism, money that was meant for family needs, children's education, or retirement savings. They find themselves at risk for sexually transmitted infections from partners whose sexual activities they knew nothing about. They experience profound betrayal trauma from discovering that their most intimate relationship was built on systematic deception.

Children become unwitting victims when they accidentally discover pornographic material on family computers, witness inappropriate sexual behavior, or grow up in homes destabilized by the chaos that sexual addiction creates. They never chose to have their sense of safety and security undermined by a parent's compulsive sexual behavior, yet they bear the psychological and developmental consequences for years or even decades.

Coworkers and colleagues suffer when workplace environments become hostile due to sexual harassment, inappropriate sexual conduct, or the professional fallout from sexual misconduct scandals. They never agreed to work in environments where their safety, comfort, or career advancement might be compromised by someone else's sexual compulsions.

Community members find their institutions, whether churches, schools, civic organizations, damaged by sexual scandals involving leaders whose addictive behavior destroys trust and effectiveness. Congregation members who invested their faith and resources in religious institutions, students whose educational environment becomes disrupted, and citizens whose civic organizations lose credibility all suffer consequences they never chose.

The concept of consent, which is fundamental to healthy sexuality, becomes meaningless when addiction drives behavior that systematically impacts others without their knowledge or agreement. Sexual addiction creates a web of involuntary participants: people whose lives, relationships, financial security, physical health, emotional well-being, and future opportunities become collateral damage in someone else's compulsive sexual behavior.

Perhaps most tragically, many of these unwilling participants initially blamed themselves for problems they didn't cause. Spouses wondered if they were "enough" sexually, children thought they had done something wrong to cause family tension, and coworkers questioned whether they had somehow invited inappropriate behavior. The true scope of their victimization often only becomes clear when the addiction is finally exposed.

This involuntary involvement of others distinguishes sexual addiction from consensual adult sexual behavior and explains why it cannot remain a "private matter." When compulsive sexual behavior inevitably draws unwilling participants into its orbit, it becomes a public concern requiring intervention, treatment, and protection for those who never consented to be part of someone else's sexual acting-out.

- **Prevention Is Possible**

  Understanding sexual addiction as a public health issue enables us to develop prevention strategies, education programs, and early intervention approaches that can reduce its prevalence and impact. When we recognize that sexual addiction affects all of us, we can work together to address its root causes and provide support for those affected.

  A public health approach would focus on primary prevention through comprehensive sexual education that teaches healthy sexuality, consent, and emotional regulation skills before problems develop. This includes age-appropriate education about the risks of early pornography exposure, media literacy to help young people critically evaluate sexual content, and trauma-informed approaches that address the childhood experiences that create vulnerability to sexual addiction.

  Secondary prevention involves early identification and intervention when problematic patterns begin to emerge, such as screening for compulsive sexual behavior in healthcare settings, training educators and counselors to recognize warning signs, and providing accessible treatment resources before behaviors escalate to the level of full addiction.

  Community-wide approaches could include policy changes that limit children's access to pornographic content, workplace education about maintaining appropriate boundaries, and public awareness campaigns that reduce stigma while encouraging people to seek help. When entire communities understand sexual addiction as a treatable condition rather than a shameful moral failing, individuals are more likely to seek help before their behavior destroys relationships and institutions. Changes such as these are possible, as evidenced by the way we now understand and treat alcoholism, once also viewed as a matter of morality and weakness.

- **Our Children's Future**

Perhaps most importantly, we must care about sexual addiction because our children are growing up in a world where addictive sexual content is more available and normalized than ever before. The choices we make today about how to address sexual addiction will determine whether future generations grow up with healthy understandings of sexuality or whether they inherit a world where sexual exploitation and addiction are simply accepted as normal.

Sexual addiction is not a private matter because its consequences are never truly private. When we understand the extensive ways that compulsive sexual behavior affects families, institutions, and society, we can begin to address it with the seriousness and comprehensive approach it deserves. The cost of ignoring sexual addiction is simply too high: for individuals, families, and society as a whole.